THE BIG DECISION

A Story and Framework to Inspire and Empower Better Life Decisions

by Zach Friedland and Daniel Friedland, MD

Published by SuperSmartHealth Publishing.

Neither the publisher nor authors are engaged in rendering professional advice or
services to the individual reader. The ideas, practices and suggestions contained
in this book are not intended to diagnose, treat, prevent or cure any disease, or to
provide specific medical advice, nor are they intended as a substitute for consulting
with your physician or other healthcare provider. Any questions regarding your
health should be directed to a qualified health practitioner. Neither the authors nor
publisher shall be liable or responsible for any loss or damage allegedly arising
from any information or suggestion in this book.

ISBN-13: 978-1484029909
ISBN-10: 1484029909

P.O. Box 910286
San Diego, CA 92191-0286
Telephone: 858-481-2393
Email: info@supersmarthealth.com

For Sue and Dylan

TABLE OF CONTENTS

Part 1: The Story of a Big Decision

Part 2: A Framework for Your Big Decisions

COMPANION WEBPAGE

Thank you for reading our book!

To get extra bonus material and join our community to support each other to make better life decisions go to

TheBigDecisionBook.com

Please also review the book on Amazon so we can make future versions even better.

Many Thanks!

PREFACE

One of the most important skills you can have and teach others is how to make good decisions in life. These lessons are especially important around the transition into adulthood where you begin making decisions that affect the rest of your life.

This book is a collaboration between a father and son sharing how to make better life decisions. Hopefully it will inspire mothers and fathers to share this with their sons and daughters too.

In the first section of the book, Zach, who began writing this when he was 12, tells a story of Ryan, who is facing a big decision. After struggling with it, Ryan approaches his father, hoping he will make the decision for him. But his dad takes a different approach, pointing out that he's arrived at the stage in his life where he needs to learn how to make good decisions for himself. Instead of making the decision for Ryan, his father gives Ryan something more important – a framework that he can use to make his own decisions.

The story in the first part of the book is written for teenagers and will hopefully entertain and inspire adults too.

In the second part of the book, Daniel, who is Zach's real life father, clarifies the 4-Step Framework Ryan's father gave Ryan to help him make his big decision. Daniel, like Ryan's father in the book, is a physician. He wrote one of the early textbooks on Evidence-Based Medicine, a framework all doctors now use to make medical decisions. In this section of the book Daniel has adapted and integrated this framework with an understanding of how your brain works to empower you to make better life decisions.

The second part of the book is written for adults who would like to learn how to make better decisions for themselves, as well as share these lessons by discussing this section of the book with their children too. While this part of the book delves into brain science and practices of how to work and rewire your brain to make better decisions, many teens may connect directly with this section too.

This book can also help counselors, coaches or teachers who want to advise their clients, team members or students how to make better life decisions.

The 4-Step Framework can also be used to inspire and empower leaders and employees to work together to make better decisions at work.

We have set up a webpage where you can find additional resources and become part of a community that shares and learns from each other how this framework can be used to make challenging life decisions. You'll also find a video here of Zach and Daniel sharing why they are so excited to share this book with you. Please visit the website at: TheBigDecisionBook.com

PART 1

The Story of a Big Decision
By Zach Friedland and Daniel Friedland, MD

CHAPTER 1

FAMILY, FOOTBALL AND FALL

"Hut, hut, hike!" Ryan said. His dirty blonde hair waved as he heaved the football back through his legs to Justin, his soon-to-be uncle. Ryan sprinted full speed to the end of the yard, turned and leaped to catch the ball with his thin but strong arms. As he came down with it, they both yelled, "TOUCHDOWN!"

It was a typical fall day in Benton: the crisp, cool air caused the town to slow down even more. If it weren't for football season, Ryan was sure that not much else would be happening in the small town in Pennsylvania after the first of September.

Fall's colored leaves floated from the trees lining his Aunt's backyard, but there was still plenty of space to practice a few plays. Several other families were playing ball around their backyards as well. Football was one of the town's favorite pastimes. Ryan loved visiting his Aunt Sarah and practicing his plays with Justin.

Justin was a former NFL linebacker for the Chicago Bears, who happened to be engaged to Ryan's favorite Aunt, Sarah.

Unfortunately, he only played for three years before he blew out his knee.

But he was still great at football. He was the best linebacker on his high school and college football teams. He was quick on his feet, strong, and seemed to know which way the ball was going on the field before the play actually happened.

He injured his knee tackling an opponent during one of the biggest games of his career – a playoff game between the Chicago Bears and the Minnesota Vikings. His knee never fully recovered, so he was released from his contract, ending his NFL career.

Although he was disappointed, he also saw it as an opportunity to help others and accepted a job as a high school football coach. Ryan hoped that next year, after he graduated from middle school, Justin would be his coach. He also wanted his math teacher to be his Aunt Sarah. Justin was the best coach, and Sarah was the best teacher at the local high school.

Ryan thought of Justin as a mentor. Justin taught him everything he knew about playing football, from how to set up and make plays to how to anticipate the other team's plays and instinctively respond.

"Nice throw, Ryan; that was amazing!" Aunt Sarah appeared, smiling at them from the porch. Her tall frame barely missed the hummingbird feeder. Ryan couldn't wait until he was taller than his aunt, but for now at 5 foot 4, he was still almost a half-foot shorter. Sarah kept telling him he would have his big growth spurt in high school.

She just got home from her job and was still wearing her "old lady teacher clothes," as Ryan called them.

"How did you get home so early, Justin?" Sarah asked. While she and Justin taught at the same school, they didn't always keep the same schedule.

"There was no practice today, honey, so I got to pick Ryan up from school to play ball with him," Justin replied.

"Oh, nice! I bet Ryan's giving you a great workout," she said, giving Ryan a wink. "Seriously, I'm so glad I got to see your game last week. You were so good!"

"Oh, thanks. Also, I really appreciate the Eagles football jersey you gave me. That jersey is so sick," Ryan replied.

"You're welcome. I loved watching your big score!" said his aunt. Sarah and Justin made it to almost every game Ryan played.

"Yeah, nice job on that touchdown, especially the way you juked out that lineman and outran the safety. You should have heard Aunt Sarah; she was cheering so loud for you I thought I'd bust an eardrum," Justin said.

"Thanks, but I think I could have done better on defense. I missed a few tackles. I wish I could tackle just like you in your game films from college and the pros. Do you think you could give me some more tips on the technique?" Ryan asked.

"Oh yeah, sure, champ, but first let's go inside and have a snack. I'm starved."

"I'll make some sandwiches," Sarah said. She, Justin, and Ryan walked into the spacious, open kitchen. Ryan loved the way Sarah's kitchen was always well stocked with snacks for him. Sarah poured three glasses of milk and took out ingredients for grilled cheese sandwiches. Justin and Ryan plopped on the big, leather sofa in the adjoining family room and flipped on the 60-inch flat-screen TV to ESPN.

A few minutes later, Sarah came in with three grilled cheese sandwiches. She sat down next to Justin.

"So, I finally got the cake order in today. I decided to go with the Spanish lemon cake," Sarah said, taking a big bite of her sandwich.

"Great!" Justin said, happily.

Ryan knew that Justin didn't care what kind of cake he had at the wedding. He just wanted to marry Sarah. The wedding was for her, and he wanted to be supportive. "The big day's coming! Hey, Ryan, are you ready to replace that football jersey with a suit and tie and stand next to me on my big day?"

"You got it! I can't wait for you to be my uncle," he replied. The wedding was just a short few weeks away.

"It's going to be an amazing day, and we are so lucky that you will be a part of it." Ryan's aunt gave him a warm glance.

"I know! It will be AWESOME!"

CHAPTER 2

THE PLAYOFFS

"Red, set, go!" shouted the quarterback for the Dolphins, the opposing team. Lining up against players wearing red and black, Ryan's team, the Tigers, wearing maroon and gold, shone brightly in the sun, ready to make a stop. This could be the last game of the season. It was the quarterfinals of the playoffs. Lose and you're done. The Tigers, were trailing 7-0 with ten minutes left in the fourth quarter.

Oh no! Ryan thought. *We're in trouble!* But even though they were down, Ryan decided he had to stay optimistic about the game. This was Ryan's first year playing football, and he loved it. In fact, he had been dreaming of playing football since he was five, but his parents didn't allow him to play until this year because he was too small. Still, this didn't stop him from fantasizing and playing pickup games at school or with his friends. When he finally started growing and catching up to others in his class, his parents reconsidered and he was allowed to join the Tigers with a bunch of other rookie players.

"Okay, boys, we're still in this game. Let's move that ball!"

Coach Johnson exclaimed. "Let's block for Jack and turn this thing around!" Even though this was not the best team he'd coached, Coach Johnson was great at motivating his team to do their best and they played their hearts out for him.

It was an added bonus that Ryan got to practice with Justin on the side and made such rapid progress in his game.

Ryan was the second string running back. In tryouts Coach Johnson could see he was quick, strong, agile and dependable to move the ball. He exceeded his coaches' expectations, but still he wasn't as good as his teammate and best friend, Jack, the first string running back. Jack was an amazing player. He could do everything – cut, run, juke. He was fast and quick, he had the strength to plow through the opposing team, and he could outrun anyone in the division.

The Dolphins kicked off after their touchdown and conversion. Jack received the kickoff and, after juking 5 defenders, ran it back to the Dolphins' twenty-two-yard line. The Tigers were well positioned, and after Coach's pep talk and Jack's fantastic kickoff return, the Tigers were feeling pumped.

On the Tigers' first offensive play, Jack took the ball and ran up the middle for a three-yard gain. Ryan subbed in and tried to run around the outside, but got smothered in the backfield. Jack came back in and got a pitch on the outside, cut right, broke left, spun, then sped down the sideline. He scored! Touchdown Tigers! The conversion was good and now the score was tied, 7-7.

The game remained tied until late in the fourth quarter when the Dolphins made a fifty-yard run down the sideline and brought the ball to the Tigers' five-yard line.

The Tigers were furious they'd given up such a big play. There was just no way they were going to give in after fighting so hard to come back. At the scrimmage line, they were amped up and ready to let loose. They went all out, swarming and crushing the Dolphins' ball carrier. He was hit so hard that he dropped the ball. The forced fumble was recovered by the Tigers!

There were 18 seconds left, time for maybe two or three plays.

"Red, set, go!" the Tigers' quarterback, Josh, yelled to start the play. Josh heaved it deep to Jack, who was streaking down the sideline. He caught it and somehow made it to the Tigers 43-yard line!

The Tigers called a time-out to discuss what would happen next. "Just run out the time, boys! Hold onto that ball and don't let ANYONE take it from you. We'll run out the clock and go for the win in overtime," advised Coach Johnson. "Ryan, you'll get the handoff. And hold onto that ball like your life depends on it!"

"Red, set, go," Josh called. Ryan, number 42 for the Tigers, ran towards the right, opened his hands, received the football and found the hole between the tackle and tight end. The Dolphins safety immediately dove at him and went for his knees. But as Ryan was building up speed, he anticipated this move and leapt up, hurdling the safety. He was clear! He landed solidly and took off down the sideline as fast as he could, outrunning the other defenders, into the end zone.

TOUCHDOWN! Ryan scored the winning touchdown! No one could believe it!

(To watch the video of this play, go to:
TheBigDecisionBook.com/video1)

Ryan was in a state of shock and joy when Jack grabbed him by the face-mask and exclaimed, "YEAH! Great job, Ryan! That was an unbelievable play! You just gave us the win! Now we are going to the semis. You're the man!" Then, the rest of the team swarmed in to dogpile Ryan.

From the corner of his eye, Ryan saw Coach Johnson approach with a big, broad smile on his face. "Pizza! Everyone gets pizza on me!" Coach Johnson's offer was met with a chorus of cheering.

Later at the pizza parlor, Coach Johnson gave an arousing victory speech. "Congratulations, guys! That was a huge win.

You guys really played your hearts out. You left it all on the field. Outstanding effort! I can't believe you guys won – that was a very tough team. They were bigger and better than us physically, but you wanted it more. You had heart and determination! Remember that feeling because now we're moving on – we qualify for the semifinals!"

Ratcheting up his intensity, Coach Johnson cautioned, "Celebrate tonight, but know that we're not done yet! Next week, it's going to be the hardest game you'll ever play this season. We are playing the number one seed, the Hornets, for a spot in the finals. They won the championship last year, and they're looking forward to defending it again this year. You guys will have to bring your 'A' game. If we lose, we're out. But if we win, we get to play in the championship match, two weeks from now!"

"Now, let's celebrate with some pizza," he said, while taking a big bite of pizza. Everybody dug in. The noise from everyone's excitement erupted around him.

But while all of Ryan's teammates were celebrating, he was deep in thought.

He hadn't imagined they'd make it this far. Their team was the 6th seed of the 8 contenders.

Uh oh, thought Ryan, *two weeks on Saturday? This could be a huge problem. The championship game is the same day as Aunt Sarah's wedding!* Ryan's excitement about scoring the winning touchdown and advancing in the playoffs suddenly turned into worry. What was he going to do?

As the team wolfed down pizza and gulped their sodas, post-game banter excitedly flew around the table. "That was so awesome, guys!" "I can't believe we won! That was so cool!" "I can't wait to play the next game!" "What if we win the next game? We'll be in the championship then. That'd be crazy!" chattered the boys.

"Did you see that play in the third quarter? I knocked that guy out of his shoes! He fell flat on his back!" said Nick, a stocky kid known for crushing opponents in impressive tackles.

"Oh yeah, that was so sick! I loved the play when you blocked that kid and I was able to cut back to the other side and get that first down on 3rd and 8!" Nate, another first-year team member, said to Ryan.

"Wait, guys, but we're playing the Hornets! They won the championship last year, and they are the best team in the league. I don't know if we can beat them. We're outmatched. We're the underdogs. They're so good – I saw their game film from last year where they crushed the Cougars, 42-0, in the championship," explained Brandon. He was the team pessimist. Whenever the rest of the team had their heads in the sky, his feet were firmly planted to Earth with facts and statistics.

Whew, that's a relief. I don't really want to win the next game, thought Ryan, *because I'd be in tough spot with my aunt's wedding. I don't want to miss either of them. It would suck to miss the game, but it would really be bad to miss my aunt's wedding. Both Sarah and Justin really need me there.*

Coach Johnson approached the table while Ryan was in mid-thought and said to everyone, "Again, great job guys! You all played an outstanding game! Josh, you had some great passes and quarterbacked well. Jack you had some really sweet runs out there. Tim, nice fumble recovery! And Ryan, what a great game! That was one of the best games I've seen you play. If anything ever happened to Jack, I know we'll be able to rely on you to pull us through."

He always went into grand speeches at least twice every post-game. When they won, he would rile them up and give praise, but even if they lost, he'd never put them down. He'd just find a way to fire them up to do better the next game.

Coach Johnson was a demanding, but encouraging and fair coach. He had a goatee and always covered his bald head with his New England Patriots cap. He had a rough, booming voice, wore a stopwatch and a whistle around his neck, and carried a clipboard wherever he went.

Every day, no matter what the weather was, he wore his usual long black shorts and his grey T-shirt with the Tigers logo on his chest. Back in high school and college, he was a defensive lineman. His playing style was much different from Ryan's. Ryan played with agility and speed, while Ryan had heard his coach played like Nick and had a special talent for plowing through his opponents.

Coach Johnson demanded one hundred percent effort from his team. There was no excuse for missing or being late to a game or a practice. While he motivated his team, he didn't give compliments freely, so his comments today really meant something.

Wow, thought Ryan. *Coach is really depending on me. I didn't think I was that important to the team, but they're all depending on me. If we win the next game, I don't know if I could miss the final game after all. Aww, man, what should I do? I mean, I can't disappoint my team and let them down. However, I can't miss the wedding.*

Is it possible to do both? The team continued to talk excitedly in the background, but Ryan was too distracted, wrestling with his own predicament to add to the commotion.

But then again, we probably won't win anyway and I won't have to worry about it. And they have Jack to lead the team, anyway.

This thought thankfully snapped him back to the present. Ryan decided that he would just enjoy the victory and stop thinking about problems that might not even happen. He grabbed a slice of pizza and joined in on the conversation by complimenting Jack on his brilliant 38-yard catch that helped set up Ryan's game-winning play.

CHAPTER 3

CONFLICTED IN THE CAFETERIA

Ryan sat with his friends in a typical middle school cafeteria: giant lunch lines of kids filing by with trays of food served by hair-netted lunch ladies, and a cash register at the end. The scent of sloppy joes, French fries, and pizza filled the cafeteria. Dozens of tables were packed together, crowded with hundreds of kids.

"Dude, the playoffs are going to be so fun. What if we beat the next team? Then we will get to play in the championships," said Nate.

"Yeah, I know! That will be so awesome! I hope we win!" said Josh.

But instead of joining in their excitement, this again triggered Ryan's conflict. It felt like it was beginning to tear him apart.

"Hey, what's wrong, Ryan? You usually talk the most," said Jack.

"What?" Ryan exclaimed, caught in his distraction. "Oh,

nothing," he said.

"No, Ryan, seriously, what's wrong? You look out of it," said Jack.

"I'm just worried I might have a wedding to go to if we make it to the championship game," he said, immediately stuffing his mouth with French fries to keep from having to answer further.

"Are you serious?" asked Nick.

"Well, maybe," Ryan mumbled with his mouth still full of food.

"Yeah right, really Ryan, you're just messing with us, right?" Jack asked.

"I'm afraid not," Ryan said, wishing he hadn't said anything in the first place.

"Come on, Ryan. We need you on our team. We can't win without you," pleaded Josh, the team's quarterback.

"We'd lose! We have nobody else as good as you or Jack," said Brandon.

"Don't worry," Ryan responded. "You've got Jack. He is way better than me. And he'll be good to go!"

"Yeah, but what if something happens to him?" asked Nate, "Is there any way you'd be able to miss that wedding? I mean for us?"

"Well, I don't know. I think I'd have to go to the wedding because she is like a mother to me and she does stuff for me and she cares for me and… Besides, this probably won't become a problem at all," said Ryan

"What do you mean?" asked Brandon.

"We don't even know if we will play in the championship game anyway. We still have to get through the Hornets. That's going to be the best team we'll ever play," said Ryan.

"Oh yeah, the Hornets. They blew out the Cougars in the championship last year. They are going to be tough. We need to make a plan to stop them," said Brandon.

"Did anyone see any film on them? Does anybody know any of their plays?" asked Ryan.

"Well, I know that they always try to run outside and they have most of their defensive players on the inside," said Nick.

"Great! We can just run outside the line of scrimmage and spread our players on the outside," said Josh.

"That's a good idea," said Ryan, again getting caught up in the excitement of the game. Everyone, including him, forgot about his potential conflict as they chatted away, scheming about game plans and cracking jokes at the lunch tables.

CHAPTER 4

GRIT AND GLORY

Ryan looked out at the dark, stormy clouds building in the distance. The light was low, breaking through the dawn. He felt the significance of the day as the trees groaned and the grass rustled in the wind. This was game day. The Hornets stood between the Tigers and the championship game.

As Ryan arrived in the parking lot of the stadium, he was relieved to see Jack climbing out of his car. "You ready, Ryan? It's game day. Let's go and kick some butt," said Jack.

"I guess so," Ryan said, nervous for the game. Ryan felt intimidated, and could tell that today was going to be a real battle.

Jack, optimistic as always, exclaimed, "Then let's go!" And they both started jogging to the far end of the field where their team was. As they did, they had to pass the opposing team, and man, did they look tough!

Somehow when you're nervous, everything looks scarier. They were towering like giants over the field compared to Ryan's team. "Look at the size of these dudes, Jack!" Ryan whispered. "I wouldn't be surprised if one of them could take a five-yard step." The Hornets had started running in their warm-ups. They were just jogging, but Ryan could see they had the speed of sprinters and the power of wrestlers. Overall, he knew this was going to be the best team they had ever played. They were a scary good team.

Ryan and Jack ran past the menacing-looking giants and joined their team. As they arrived, Coach Johnson, with his clipboard in hand, motioned for everyone to gather together. He could sense that his team was feeling a little intimidated and could do with a little firing up.

"Let's go, guys! This is our game; it is not our day to lose! We are going to score first and our defense will stop them. As big as they look, you'll find a way to feel that determination you felt last game and crush them! No matter what happens, do not give up. If they score, hold your heads high and then we will score right back. It doesn't matter how big they are, how strong, or how fast they are. We have more heart, intensity and effort. If you guys want to keep playing football, you will have to leave it all on the field, put your hearts into it and give your best effort!"

Coach Johnson had worked his magic. The energy level intensified and warm-ups flew by. Soon the Tigers were on the field, ready to do battle.

Jack, Brandon, and Ryan went out for the coin toss. Jack did the talking this time. He called heads as the shiny silver coin spun into the air. It landed on the ground with the tails side up. The opposing team got to call and chose to receive the ball first and to defend the north end zone.

The Tigers came out fighting. They played with heart, surprising themselves and everybody watching from the stands. Against all odds, it was a pretty even game until close to halftime. One defense would hold up the other team's offense, and then the same would happen again for the other team. Then, near the end of the second quarter, Jack had a breakaway forty-yard run. The Tigers controlled the ball and scored first! They held the lead until three minutes before the first half ended, until the Hornets got a breakaway and scored to tie the game.

Then, with thirty seconds left in the first half, the Tigers had the ball on the fifty-yard line. Jack got a pitch out to the left and started running the ball full speed down the left sideline. As he focused on getting around the corner, he didn't see #41, the Hornets' safety, sprinting across the field. Just as Jack got to the corner, he slowed up a fraction, looking for an opening. As Jack slowed, the safety leaned in and dove, driving his helmet into Jack's right knee. It twisted, and you could hear a snapping sound. Jack screamed as he crashed into the turf in pain, while the crowd gasped.

Even after ten minutes, Jack was still down. Everyone knew something serious had happened because Jack didn't pop onto his feet quickly like he usually did after a big hit. Finally, after what seemed like forever, an ambulance came. The medics put Jack's leg in a splint and took him off to the hospital.

The game clock restarted and a few seconds later ran into halftime. In silence and shock with their heads down, the Tigers shuffled off to their side of the field for the halftime break.

Ryan's team looked beaten. They'd lost their best player, and they felt like they were finished. Coach Johnson tried to lift their spirits, but this didn't seem to have its usual effect.

Feeling the energy sucked out of the team, intensity mixed with anger began to stir inside Ryan. He stepped up with a burst of newfound energy and confidence.

"Let's go, guys. We're still in this game. We may not have Jack, but we still have a team. Let's pick up our heads and start playing football. We are right where we want to be. It's a tied game. Are we going to let this defeat us, or are we going to pick ourselves up? Let's get fired up and go give it right back to them! And let's do it for Jack!"

Coach Johnson nodded with approval, knowing that this was exactly the pep talk they needed to rally. "You heard Ryan. You're not done yet. This is a time for heroes. This is a time for leaders. This is your time. Go out there. Do this for yourselves. Do this for your school. Do this for Jack!"

Heads lifted, and the team realized that the game actually wasn't over. They *were* still in this. The game was tied. They could still win. They started to pump each other up. Coach Johnson called them over to warm up their legs. They did some light ten-yard jogs and started getting ready to play again. The horn rang for them to start the second half and they jogged off the field, pumped up to play.

In the huddle, Ryan said, "Come on guys, let's go and finish this game and get to the championship for Jack!" The team huddled tightly together and in unison started jumping and shouting "Jack, Jack, Jack!" Then Ryan shouted, "Tigers on three! One, two three," and everyone bellowed, "Tigers!" They then ran over to the sideline, fired up and ready to go for the remainder of the game.

The Tigers took the field, ready to field the kickoff. The game was still a defensive battle for the Tigers. They had no success on offense, but managed to hold the Hornets when they were on offense. Still, it was an exhausting defensive battle and the Tigers were starting to get discouraged. They just didn't seem to have offensive power now that Jack was out of the game.

Then, with three minutes to go in the game, the Hornets threw a long pass that was caught twelve yards away from the end zone. Luckily, the Tigers managed to tackle the wide receiver and keep him from running into the end zone.

But the next play, the Hornets set up to throw a pass into the end zone. Out of nowhere, Nate, at safety, crossed in front of the Hornets' tight end, intercepted the ball and ran it all the way back to the Tigers 40-yard line.

Ryan felt a surge of confidence in his team. They broke the Hornets' momentum and had a real chance to win! But now they couldn't move the ball. Hope turned to concern as it became fourth down. With less than two minutes left in the game, they had to punt from their 42-yard line.

Coach Johnson called out the punt team. He still had three time-outs and still had confidence in his defense. It was a great punt. His kicker got it to the Hornets own 5-yard line.

The Tigers defense brought everything they had and shut the Hornets down on their next three plays. With only twelve seconds left, the Hornets decided to punt from their 10-yard line.

Ryan was punt returner in place for Jack. He knew what was at stake, and he was ready for this play.

Sweat dripped down Ryan's face. The punt was high. Ryan located it and took a few steps backward to get under it at the Hornets 43-yard line. His heart was pumping hard and his feet were a blur as he caught the ball and cut towards the sideline. His ears were filled with an echo of sounds from the screaming fans. He could feel the pounding footsteps of his opponents chasing him down. He saw a wall of purple defenders in front of him. It looked like two Hornets had him at the 20-yard line. Impossibly he broke these tackles, but then he saw three more Hornets come at him.

His adrenaline was surging. He found a source of strength and speed he didn't even know he had. His momentum took over and he powered through all of them. He could see the end zone gleaming in front of him. There was no more time left on the clock. This was do or die.

The whole team was counting on Ryan to make this play so they could participate in the championship game. The Tigers' friends and family were all here to see the big game. Ryan could taste the victory and flashed on the games he'd played with Justin in his Aunt Sarah's yard. Ryan felt two Hornets on his back, closing in on him. He dove for the goal line. A streak of purple flashed in front of his face. The ball was knocked out of his hands!

But not before he'd crossed the line. TOUCHDOWN!

(Watch the video! Go to:
TheBigDecisionBook.com/video2)

The crowd exploded! Cheerleaders ran down the sideline. His teammates swarmed him. Ryan was stunned. He had made an impossible winning touchdown on a punt return against a team of giants. The Tigers were going to the championship!

But then, in the height of his excitement, a sense of dread hit him. The wedding.

Now he had a big decision to make.

CHAPTER 5

A BAD BREAK

After the excitement of the game and an evening of celebrating with the team, Ryan rested on his bed, staring at the blank ceiling trying to fall asleep. But sleep wasn't coming. Thoughts raced through his head. He was happy about helping his team win, but kept wondering if Jack was going to be okay. He tried to reassure himself by imagining that it didn't look too bad.

Surely Jack's leg only twisted, so it was probably just a sprain. But then again, he couldn't get up and had to be taken to the hospital, and that was just not like Jack. He usually just popped right up, even if it was just a sprain. Could something worse have happened?

If it is worse than a sprain, what will I do? It felt so good to help my team win today, but I just can't play in the championship game. Can I? Ryan exhausted himself, locked in conflicted thoughts, and eventually fell into a fitful sleep...

Ryan looked into Jack's smiling face. They walked to their first class together. Jack talked about the accident and how nice the nurses were to him when he was in the hospital. He was concerned that he may have had a serious injury, but then the doctor came in and gave him the great news that it was just a sprain and he just needed to ice it and rest for a couple of days. The doctor said he would be okay to practice and would be fine to play in the championship.

"Ryan, I'm going to play in that game no matter what! I'll finish the game even if I get hit again," Jack said as they took their seats in class.

Ryan was so relieved to hear that Jack was okay and back to his usual determined, optimistic self. The pressure was off of him to play in the important game. Since Jack was okay to play, Ryan would be able to go to the wedding without feeling like he was letting his team down.

Then in the background he heard a ringing noise, over and over. Where was it coming from? Suddenly, he woke up. He felt like something was wrong. It was early Sunday morning and the phone was ringing downstairs. He dragged himself out of bed and trudged down the stairs. His mom was holding out the phone: "It's for you."

Ryan wondered which of his friends was calling so early in the morning.

"Hello," Ryan said into the phone.

"Hello, Ryan. It's Coach Johnson. I have some bad news." As he heard these words, Ryan's stomach dropped and his heart skipped a beat.

"What's the bad news?" Ryan had a bad feeling that his dream was not going to come true. He knew the bad news was about Jack.

"Son, Jack's dad called me last night and told me that Jack's injury is more serious than we thought. He broke his leg in two places. It's terrible news. We feel really bad for Jack and sorry he won't be able to play in the championship game. Thankfully, we still have you! Are you going to be ready to step up and play?" Coach asked.

Without even thinking, Ryan replied, "Yeah, of course, Coach! I'm always ready!" But as soon as he said these words, he felt rattled. He was uncertain. He was sad that his friend was hurt and he wanted to please his coach and be there for his team. Without thinking, he found himself reassuring his coach that he was up for it. But what his coach couldn't see over the phone was that he suddenly broke out into an anxious sweat.

"That's great, because you're the leader of the team now and we need you fully fired up if we're going to go all the way. See you at tomorrow's practice."

Ryan hung up the phone. His mind felt scrambled and his body felt heavy with the burden of conflict that weighed him down.

He walked into the living room. While he was on the phone with the coach, his parents had left to run their Sunday morning errands. He was alone, and he didn't know what to do. He was worried about Jack, but he was even more worried about his big decision. He had just told the coach he would play in a game that he knew was scheduled for the same day as his Aunt's wedding. He couldn't do both. He tried to come up with a solution, but there wasn't one.

What can I do? Ryan thought. *It sounds like my coaches and players are really depending on me. And if I don't go, my coach will feel betrayed and my teammates will feel like I let them down. Geez, even all the parents and cheerleaders are going to be mad at me. Everyone is counting on me. I wish Jack could play, but he won't be playing again for months.* Ryan continued to mull over the problems in his head and only saw the consequence of him not playing get worse.

If I'm not there when they need me and they lose the game because of that, who would still like me? The coaches probably wouldn't draft me again, because I let them down. My teammates would all reject me. There's no way they would talk to me, and I'll be all alone.

But my team doesn't understand my relationship with Sarah and Justin. They wouldn't know what to do if they were in my shoes. Well, what would they do if they were in my shoes? Most of them would probably go to the game because football means a lot to them. And this is the big Championship game. They'd never understand if I didn't play. They'd never forgive me! How could I ever show my face at school again? These thoughts of being rejected felt painful.

He felt a surge of frustration. *"How could my aunt Sarah do this? How could she not know that the wedding could land on the day of the Championship Final and not plan this better?"*

Immediately he felt guilty about being angry at his favorite aunt, but he still felt trapped. *"How can I get out of this?"* Looking for the easy way out, he began to fantasize about escaping his predicament by telling Aunt Sarah that his coach was forcing him to play. Or he could tell his coach and teammates that his parents are forcing him to go to the wedding. But he didn't feel right about lying, and this felt like the coward's way out.

Maybe it's just best that I play. With that thought, he felt a wave of relief sweep over him. *I should talk about it with Sarah and Justin and see if they'd be okay with this. Well, it's worth a shot. I will try to talk to them to see what they say.*

Still, he couldn't shake the feeling deep down that even if they said they'd be okay with this, they'd really be hoping for him to go to the wedding and be disappointed if he didn't.

He looked at the clock and realized that Aunt Sarah would be there any minute to pick him up. They'd planned to spend part of Sunday going bowling. What was he going to say to her?

CHAPTER 6

A PAINFUL DECISION

Ryan heard the sound of Sarah's car pull into the driveway. The car door slammed shut and he heard her footsteps walk toward the front door. He opened it to greet her: "Hi!"

"Hey Ryan," Aunt Sarah said. "You're still in your pajamas. I thought you would be ready to go bowling. Justin is planning to meet us in twenty minutes." Ryan looked down at his old Patriots T-shirt and favorite flannel pajama pants. He obviously couldn't go bowling in them.

"Uh... well..." Ryan stammered. He didn't know how to begin. "So.... I wanted to ask a question and hear your honest opinion."

"Okay, go get dressed and we can talk about it in the car," Sarah said, but Ryan was just trying to get the conversation over with. If Sarah got upset, the last thing he wanted was to be stuck in the car with her.

Ryan turned to head back upstairs to change into his clothes. He didn't know how the words would come out of his mouth. His mouth was so dry that he didn't know if he could get any out at all.

He had so much doubt about Sarah's reaction. *Would she be mad at him? Would she understand? Would she feel let down if he did go play in the game?* The questions swirled in his mind as he tied his shoes. He walked slowly down the stairs.

"Ready?" Sarah was a little impatient sometimes; she didn't like being late.

"Well, I actually haven't finished my breakfast. Can you give me a minute? I'm almost done," he said. He was trying to stall for a minute so he could think of what he would say.

"Okay. I'll go wait in the car and call Justin to tell him we'll be a little late."

Ryan shoveled down the rest of his scrambled eggs and washed it down by chugging a glass of milk. He saw Sarah waiting in the car and walked out to meet her.

"As you know, I have a football game, the championship game, coming up," Ryan said as he closed the door and reached for his seat belt. *Get straight to the point*, Ryan thought.

"Justin and I have been meaning to talk with you about this, too. You had such a phenomenal game, but we realize this puts the championship game on the day of our wedding."

"Yeah, it's such a bummer. Not your wedding; I mean the day that it is planned on. I'm really having a hard time with this. I can't do both, and I don't know what to do. What do you think I should do?"

"Well, Justin and I know how hard this decision is for you. Of course we want you to come to our wedding, especially because you are in it, but we know how much this football game means to you and how much you mean to the team. We can see how you must feel totally torn between the wedding and playing in the game," Sarah paused, and Ryan wasn't sure what was coming next. "Are you worried about letting your team down? Or letting Justin and me down?" She turned to look Ryan in the eye.

"Yeah, that's the main thing. I don't know how you would feel if I played in the game and I am not sure what my coach and my teammates would do if I told them I couldn't play in the game because of the wedding. Either way, it feels like I have to break a promise to someone, and I really wish I could do both."

"The coach might not be mad at me if Jack could play, but Jack broke his leg. So now the coach and the entire team are counting on me. I don't want to let them down. But I don't want to let you down, either. I feel like I'm stuck in quicksand and I can't get out." Ryan turned and looked out the window. He could see his breath on the window from the cold morning air.

"Well, Ryan, that is a really tough call. You know I want you to be in the wedding, but you can't be in two places at once, so I'd certainly understand if you decided to play in the game. But I can't make the decision for you. You have to make the choice," she said.

Amazingly, she didn't look upset.

Ryan heard Sarah's words and felt relieved that she was so calm and understanding. But rather than helping him make up his mind, her being so nice and understanding only made him feel more conflicted.

Sarah and Ryan got to the bowling alley. Despite several rounds of bowling, Ryan was unable to really relax. He had too much on his mind and felt the burden of his decision. Either way, he had to figure out the choice he needed to make... and painfully soon!

He felt completely overwhelmed and completely at a loss for what to do next. He needed his parents' help. Silently he hoped they'd take the burden off his shoulders and just make the decision for him by telling him what he had to do.

CHAPTER 7

DISCOVERING HOW TO DECIDE

"Hi Ryan, where have you been?" asked his mom as she gave him a big hug. As she leaned in to give him a kiss, he artfully dipped his head and her lips met with his hair instead of his cheek. Ryan grabbed a handful of the apple slices she had been cutting up for a snack.

"Hey son, how are you doing? What's up?" Ryan's dad asked as he sat on the couch in his day-off clothes, flipping through a stack of medical journals. Late Sunday afternoon was the time he typically set aside to try and catch up on his reading.

Ryan's Dad was a doctor in internal medicine who worked long hours seeing patients.

"Oh, um, nothing," Ryan replied, not sure he was ready yet to talk about the difficult decision he had to make.

"You look like something's bothering you. Are you sure?" asked his mom.

"Well, actually I've spent last evening and today thinking

about this really painful decision I have to make. I'm hoping you can help me. Aunt Sarah's wedding is this week, and I need help deciding whether to go to her wedding or the football game."

"We've been waiting for you to raise that issue, Ryan," said his Mom, settling in on the couch next to her husband. "What are you thinking about doing?"

"Yes, Ryan, Mom and I have been discussing it. We were hoping you would come to us about it. So I'm glad you brought it up so we can talk more about it. I have to admit that really sounds like a tough decision, and I imagine how difficult this must be for you. How would you like us to help you out on your decision?" asked his Dad.

"Well, what should I do?" Ryan said, taking a seat on the ottoman in front of the couch to face his parents. He was hoping they would give him an easy way out and make the decision for him.

"Ryan, I know Sarah would understand if you can't make the wedding, but we won't make this decision for you either way. You're getting to the age where it's really important to know how to begin making difficult decisions for yourself. You're going to face a lot of situations where you need to make a tough decision, and you have to learn how to do it."

"While I won't tell you what decision to make, I can share with you a way to make this and other decisions for yourself," his dad said.

This was not the answer Ryan had expected. He braced, realizing there was no way around this. Feeling the weight of responsibility Ryan took a deep breath and responded, "Okay, where do I start?"

"Well, you already have," his dad remarked.

"What do you mean?" he asked.

"You are asking some good questions. Making a good decision first begins with framing good questions," his father replied.

"Hmm. What are some good questions I could ask?"

"That's a great question to start with!" said his Dad.

"Other questions involve asking whether you've thought through all of your alternatives and what are the consequences of each – not only in the short term, but the long term, too."

"It's also important to think about the people who'll be affected by your decision and who is most important to you in your life. Also, how does your decision line up with your long-term goals and what you value most?"

Ryan had already been thinking about some of these questions, but having them defined now would really help him understand what was most important for him.

Ryan pondered these questions nodding, "These are helpful Dad. Just want to make sure I have them all. So first I ask what are my choices and what are the consequences of each, and who will be most affected by those choices. Then I ask how each choice fits into what I value most. And I think about the short and long term effects of my choice."

"You've got it, son! These questions are a great place to start and you may think of others as you begin to ask them."

"Okay. Then what do I do?"

"What do you do with questions?" his dad asked.

Ryan thought a moment. Was this a trick question? The answer seemed too simple: "Find the answers?"

"Right! Sometimes you can answer the questions right away, but sometimes, especially with tough decisions, you have to think about it for a while. Also, when you feel stressed out, it can scramble your brain. It feels like your brain is not working properly. It's important to find a good way to calm yourself down first so that you can think more clearly and allow your answers to find you."

Ryan could connect with this. He was really stressed out about this decision and was having a difficult time seeing things clearly and finding any answers.

"So do you have any suggestions how I can find a way to calm down and better figure things out?"

"Yes. There are a number of things that can help. You can find a peaceful spot that helps you relax. Or do something active that can take the edge off the stress for you."

"What helps you when you get stressed out, Ryan?" his Dad explored.

"Well, when I get upset I like to go for a run around the neighborhood. This usually seems to calm me down. Also, my room is my peaceful spot. It helps me to shut the door, where I can get away and lie on my bed thinking."

"That's great! There's one more thing that can also help. It's what I do when I get stressed out," shared his Dad. "It's also what I teach my patients to better deal with their stress."

"All I do is just get into a quiet place, then simply watch my thoughts and feelings in my body without judging them.

Kind of like watching clouds move across the sky. And then I just bring my attention to my breathing and breathe in a slow and relaxed way."

"How do you do that?" asked Ryan.

"You breathe in slowly over about 5 seconds and out slowly over 5 seconds or so. You keep your belly soft and simply notice how it expands when you breathe in and sinks back in when you breathe out. Try this for yourself now. Put your hand on your belly and allow yourself to just breathe in and out slowly."

"I see what you mean," said Ryan. "My hand moves out away from my body as I breathe in and then moves back in as I breathe out."

"Yes, exactly!" said his Dad.

He then went into one of his doctor-type explanations.

"There's a lot of scientific research to show that this practice works and why. This type of breathing calms the part of our nervous system that makes us feel stressed and helps us to think more clearly."

"Wow, Dad. That's amazing! I feel calmer doing this already!" Ryan couldn't believe it. He'd discovered a new way to calm himself down.

"I think this will help me to relax and find some of the answers I need."

This insight triggered Ryan's next question.

"Okay, but, once I find an answer, how do I know it's the right one?" he asked. He didn't know how he would know. That was part of his problem.

"That's another great question, Ryan!" His dad was

excited that Ryan was getting how this decision-making process worked.

"In the next step of this process you evaluate your answer. You know the answer is right if it feels right in your brain, heart and gut. You do this by asking yourself, 'Does it feel right?' rather than only focusing on, 'Does it feel good?'"

His dad paused, not sure that Ryan was getting this last part, and thought of an example. Ryan's mother then jumped in: "Like that time when you ate a bunch of your Halloween candy before dinner and you were too full to eat your nice, healthy dinner. You felt kind of sick afterward. The candy felt really good, but you knew it wasn't good to build a strong, healthy body. You know that if you only ate candy all the time and not healthy food, it would not be good for you in the long run. Eating something healthy – while it may not taste as good as candy in the moment – is the right thing to do because it is good for you over the long term."

"Oh, now I get it. Thanks, Mom!" You have to do the right thing, not necessarily the thing that feels good in the short term, Ryan thought, remembering the candy incident. The candy had tasted good in the moment, but he had no energy later and his stomach felt sick and wobbly the rest of the night. He thought how eating healthy made sense and felt like the right thing to do.

Ryan's Dad smiled at his wife. He'd run through this process a few times before with her when he'd been stuck with a difficult decision, and appreciated her knack for getting to the heart of the matter.

He then nodded to his son: "You got it, Ryan! When you only

focus on what feels good, sometimes you can get led astray in the decisions you make. If someone says to you, 'Try this drug because you'll feel good,' and you remember to ask yourself, 'Does it feel right, rather than just feel good?' hopefully you'll make a better decision and say, 'No, thanks.' Focusing on what feels right keeps you on track with what you know is healthy for you and important in your life."

"Okay, thanks! So I know to focus more on what feels right than only on what feels good. After I figure this out, what do I do next?"

"The next step is to apply your answers and decision to your situation. In this case, you're going to have to tell some people that you're letting them down. It's going to be hard, but I know you'll come up with the right decision for you. You're going to have to dig deep, find your courage and willpower to do this. And, just like when you go into your big games, be sure you're well rested, well fed and hydrated and have practiced in your mind what you want to say."

His mother added, "This won't be easy, Ryan, but we'll support whatever decision you make."

Ryan was relieved to know that he had his parents' support in working through this and would stand behind his decision. And he really appreciated that he now had a clearer way to go ahead and make his decision.

They'd covered a lot in the conversation. So, just to be sure he got everything, he checked by asking, "Okay, guys, let me get this straight. To make a good decision, first, you ask good questions. Second, you get into a good space so you can find the answers that lead you to your decision. Third, you evaluate your answers and decision to make sure it feels 'right.' And fourth, you take action on what you've decided. Did I miss anything?" Ryan wanted to clarify the process. He wanted to make sure he'd make the best possible decision.

His parents briefly glanced at each other, a bit taken aback in awe. "That's right, Ryan," his dad responded with a big smile. "It's amazing you get this. It usually takes me a lot longer to explain this to some of my patients."

"Thanks, Dad. Thanks, Mom. You really helped me out a lot." Ryan stood up. "I'm going to work through each of these steps now and see if I can make a good decision with this. Thanks again, guys!"

Ryan left the room determined. Tonight he was going to figure out which event he was going to attend. He had to. He had football practice tomorrow, and the championship game and wedding were less than a week away!

CHAPTER 8

WORKING THE DECISION

*O*kay, *I know this is going to be a very difficult choice, but I really need to decide this tonight.*

Ryan decided to go upstairs to find some quiet space to think through his questions. He took three deep breaths as he entered his room. He then climbed onto his bed, resting his back against his headboard, drew his knees towards his chest, closed his eyes and took 3 more deep, slow breaths. He began asking himself the key questions he'd clarified for himself with his dad.

Okay, so what are my alternatives? Is there any way I could do both? Can I fly down and make the wedding after the game? There's just no way. They're pretty much at the same time. I couldn't even make it if I beamed myself down. So that's not going to work.

Then he flashed, *Maybe I could ask Aunt Sarah to postpone the wedding a day or two?* He felt guilty almost as quickly as he thought this, realizing all the planning it must have taken and how everyone attending would have to change their plans. So, there was no way he was going to ask for this.

There was simply no alternative. Either he was going to play or he was going to the wedding.

Ryan took a deep breath, exhaled, and then took another deep breath, anticipating his next question. *Okay then, what are the consequences of each of these decisions?*

He first thought of all the fallout if he decided to go to the wedding. He'd already been thinking about all these ramifications and was well primed for the fear and dread this instantly triggered in him again. He replayed the movie in his mind of the reactions of shock, anger and disappointment his coach and teammates would express when he shared this decision with them. This turned to sadness and pain when he imagined that they would reject him and not speak to him for weeks and perhaps months to come. He thought about how his reputation would be trashed. He'd have no friends, and even worse, he'd be mocked and hated at school. It felt painful.

With all these frightening thoughts and feelings, he felt a sudden spike in his anxiety and almost started hyperventilating. *There's just no way I can do this. I have to play. My aunt will understand*, he thought. He felt some relief with this decision and a weight lifting off his shoulders as he imagined himself playing with his teammates.

But even through this relief felt good, something underneath still didn't feel quite right. Rather than his relief expanding, he noticed that something deep inside was gnawing at him. It churned into restlessness, and his discomfort and agitation started growing again.

He flashed, *I gotta get out of here and go for a run.* Then, just as he was about to get up and put on his running shorts and shoes, he remembered again what his dad had shared with him about the soft belly breathing.

He lay down on his bed. He noticed all of the feelings, thoughts and sensations in his body just like his dad said, viewing them like clouds passing across the sky. He then put his hand on his belly and brought his attention to his breath. He noticed as he gently breathed in how his hand rose with his belly expanding and as he breathed out how it fell.

He also noticed his thoughts and feelings, but rather than trying to fix them or make them go away, he just brought his attention back to his breath.

Ryan continued doing this for about 5 minutes. Each time his thoughts or feelings tried to grab his attention, he just brought his attention back to his breath.

He then began to notice how much more relaxed he felt and that he could think more clearly. He realized that he was not yet done making his decision.

He needed to think through the consequences of playing in the championship game and missing the wedding. He asked himself, *What would it feel like if he was not at the wedding? I'd feel so guilty about missing Sarah's wedding because she means so much to me. She's a big influence in my life and shares in my big achievements and events. Shouldn't I also share in hers? I know she'd be upset with me even if she said she wouldn't be.*

He then saw the loving faces of his family standing on the beach on this joyous day. At the same time he sensed Sarah's, Justin's and his parents' sadness and disappointment at him not being there.

He noticed how his heart ached when he saw them standing

in front of the minister on the beach, about to express their wedding vows, with a gap next to Justin where he would have been standing as best man. He felt the deep longing to be with all of them.

He then remembered something his dad had first shared with him one summer evening as they took a walk together around the neighborhood. He said he wanted to share one of the most important things his father had taught him growing up: "I want you to remember, there's nothing as important as family."

He remembered how his dad had then stopped and kneeled down in front of him and put his hands on his shoulders and said, "I also want you to know I will always love you. We are family forever." Over the years, Ryan found himself coming back to the memory of this over and over. It had especially comforted him when he had felt sad, like when he'd gotten teased or hadn't been invited to a birthday party.

His Aunt Sarah and within a few days, Uncle Justin were family forever.

He knew that his parents, Sarah and Justin were the most important people in the world to him.

Ryan thought about all the things that his family had done for him over his life. He also wondered who on the team would be around for him after middle school football ended. He may still have one or two friends, but Coach won't be in his life, and most of the guys will disappear and do their own thing, too.

All of a sudden, the football game paled in comparison to what his family meant to him. Even though he was inspired by Justin, who'd played in college and made it to the pros, Ryan knew that playing football was not really his long-term goal. He also loved playing lacrosse, and that's the sport he really wanted to pursue in high school and college.

Besides, he held out hope that his coach and teammates would forgive him and that he'd have a chance to contribute to the team next year. The wedding, on the other hand, was a once-in-a-lifetime event.

Ryan now knew deeply the decision he had to make. While he was scared about what he had to do, he felt his stomach untwist and he found peace in his heart. He knew the decision that felt right.

He went downstairs to share his decision with his parents and called his Aunt Sarah for support.

He then spent the rest of the evening rehearsing in his mind what he had to do next. He'd have to dig deep and find his courage. Tomorrow was going to be the most challenging day of his young life!

CHAPTER 9

DIGGING DEEP

"Come on, Ryan, it's time to go!" Sarah called down from the bottom of the stairs. It was Monday, just 5 days before the game and wedding. Today was the day that Ryan was going to tell his team that he would not be playing in the championship game, and instead would be going to the wedding with his family.

Ryan had already shared the news with Sarah, and while she was thrilled, she also understood how difficult this was for him. She'd offered to pick him up after school and drive him to the practice. It had been excruciating avoiding his teammates and not letting on about his decision all day. He wanted to save this for the practice.

He wasn't sure if he should suit up. He decided to go in his track pants and take his gear with him in his bag. After what he was about to share, his coach might ask him to turn in his gear anyway.

"I'm coming, just a minute. I'll meet you at the car!" Ryan yelled back from his room as he gathered up his football gear.

He knew he was making the right decision by going to Sarah's wedding, but he was nervous about his teammates' and coach's reactions. They'd know something was up as soon as they saw that he wasn't suited up for practice. This thought spiked his nerves, but he'd been rehearsing for this and remembered the drill. *Just breathe.*

He could have called the coach beforehand, but he felt it was right to face up to everyone and tell them in person. Ryan knew this was going to be hard and that he had to find a way to stay emotionally strong.

Ryan climbed into Sarah's car. She looked over compassionately and asked, "How are you doing?"

Ryan sighed, "Okay." He really appreciated just the support of knowing that she cared, but he didn't want to talk on the drive over. He just wanted to sit quietly and stare out the window as he played over in his mind what he wanted to say to his coach and team. He only hoped this would come out okay.

Ryan stepped out of the car. His heart pounded and his palms were wet as he walked towards the practice field. He'd walked this path many times, but things felt like they were moving in slow motion, and the walk felt longer than usual.

He arrived at the center of the field, where the coach had assembled everybody, taking a knee as he began to run through the practice routine. There were some new plays Coach wanted to introduce for the final, including a couple of running plays for Ryan.

Just then, Coach Johnson saw Ryan. Instantly the expression changed on Coach Johnson's face and his look of alarm triggered everyone to turn and look at Ryan, too.

"Ryan!" Coach Johnson pointed at him. "Why aren't you dressed for practice?"

Ryan scanned the faces of his teammates, quietly doing his best to slow his breathing as his gaze settled on Coach Johnson. "I'm really sorry, Coach. I have some bad news."

"The only bad news I can see is that you're not dressed for practice. What's going on?" Coach said, frowning.

"Yeah, Ryan, what's going on?" another voice echoed.

Ryan's stomach tightened. He'd planned to be brief and direct and took a deep breath, which gave him the confidence to continue.

"I've had a really tough decision to make, and it hasn't been easy. It turns out that my Aunt Sarah's wedding is on the same day as the championship game."

"Is she the one who shows up to every game?" Ryan's teammate, Joe, asked.

"Yeah, she's been to every game this season. She's really happy that our team made it into the championship, but it turns out her wedding is on the same day as the big game and it's in Cape Cod, so I can't make both. I'm really sorry, guys, but I'm not going to be able to play in the game."

"Whaaaaat?" his teammates gasped. Coach Johnson dropped his clipboard in shock and stared at Ryan. Ryan reflexively looked down at the ground. He caught himself doing this, then mindfully stood straighter and breathed deeply to regain his poise. He lifted his eyes to meet the eyes of his coach.

After a few moments of stunned silence, Coach Johnson

spoke up. "Ryan, you promised me you were going to play in this game. I was really counting on you. The team was, too," he said with anger in his voice.

"I know, Coach. I'm really sorry that I broke my promise to all of you. This has been the hardest decision of my life. I've really had to dig deep. This team and this game is really important to me, but I can't do both and I can't shake the feeling that my family and this wedding are important to me too. My aunt has been like a mother to me, and she is only going to get married this one time."

Again, Ryan's comments were met with silence. But rather than it being filled with only shock, disappointment and anger, Ryan could feel a shift. They were weighing what he said.

Sensing this shift, Ryan looked from his coach toward his teammates, "Guys, I know you might be upset at me right now. I really don't want to let you down, but I feel that the same way I've had to dig deep on my decision to do what I believe is right, you guys have it in you to dig deep, too, and can win this game without me."

"Look what we all did, pulling together as a team after Jack got hurt. Coach encouraged all of us to play with our hearts, to play for Jack, and to do our best... and we did! That shows that we are a team, and that it's not just one player; it's all of us pulling together as a team. When one guy gets knocked down, the whole team rallies and fights." Ryan looked around into the eyes of each of his teammates. Some were beginning to nod slowly and look at him a bit more positively.

"The championship game, it's not about me, and it's not about Jack. It's about our team! And our team pulls together when things get tough."

Ryan paused and then said, "I remember when we started the season, I didn't have any confidence in myself, but Coach, you helped me, and Jack inspired me to be the best I can be. I want you to go out and win this game for Jack and for Coach. Have confidence in yourselves. I have confidence in you! I know you can do it," Ryan turned to meet his coach's eyes as he finished up saying all he'd come prepared to say.

"Well, it sounds like you've made up your mind. I respect you coming to tell us in person. I have to admit that I am disappointed that you won't be our star player, but you have shown your teammates an important lesson in priorities, and making a tough decision," Coach Johnson said and turned to look at the team. "There are going to be times when you boys will have to choose between things that mean a lot to you. Ryan has showed us an important lesson here about making decisions, digging deep and having confidence in yourselves."

Ryan noticed that more of his teammates were nodding in agreement with Coach. He also knew that there were some who still felt let down, and he was sorry that they didn't understand. Eventually, they would get it, too.

"Well, Ryan, I can see you need to be at the wedding, and we'll do our best without you. I appreciate that you came out here and had the courage to talk to us directly," Coach said.

"Thanks, Coach." Ryan felt a deep respect from his coach, who understood what he was going through.

"But I'm going to ask you for one thing – did you bring your gear today?"

"Yes, Coach," said Ryan quietly, thinking he would have to

turn in his gear and be kicked off the team.

"Great! Well, go and suit up. I want you to help us practice today and Wednesday. Our defense needs someone to challenge them. Besides, if there is anyone here who is still mad at you for this, it'll give them a reason to hit you extra hard in scrimmage."

"Yes, Coach!" replied Ryan.

With that, his teammates laughed. Nate shouted, "Yeah, Ryan, go get changed and come back ready to be hit."

As Ryan jogged off to the locker room to get changed, he felt the weight of the world lift off his shoulders. He had done it. He made one of the hardest decisions he ever had to make all on his own. And he expressed himself in a way that his coach and teammates still respected him. He was amazed at how this had all unfolded. And he was impressed with his newfound ability to make difficult decisions, which gave him great confidence for his future. Now, he could focus on enjoying his last few practices with his buddies – and try not to get crushed.

CHAPTER 10

THE DRIVE

A fter a happy week helping his team out at practice getting hit extra hard in scrimmage, Ryan enjoyed the car ride to Cape Cod. It was Thursday. The family decided to drive up early so they could enjoy Friday on the beach before the wedding on Saturday. It was a glorious, warm, late fall day with a clear blue sky. Ryan rode with his parents in front and Sarah and Justin in the back with him, playing several different road trip games, like spotting license plates. Later on, they listened to music from Ryan's iPod.

Ryan had no doubt that he made the right decision. Family was his most important priority. He asked himself if there was anything he needed to do further after having made his decision. What came to him was to think good thoughts and wish his team every success.

He sent a text to Jack, who would be at the game with his cast on: "on our way to cape cod...remind all to dig deep and txt me to LMK what happens during the game!"

A few seconds later, he got a reply from Jack: "you got it.

wish we were playing. have fun out there!"

Ryan smiled and nodded off. A few hours passed when Ryan was awakened by soft shaking from Sarah. "We're here, Ryan. We're in Cape Cod!" He quickly jumped out of his seat; he couldn't wait to see the beach. They arrived at the beach just in time for a beautiful burnt orange sunset that reflected off a shimmering ocean. Waves gently lapped on the sand. It was so amazing that he just kept staring.

"Wow," Ryan said. "This is awesome." As the sun faded into the horizon, so did the worries he had about his team. With his big decision behind him, he was now focusing more on Sarah's wedding and the joy of being with his extended family.

Ryan's moment of silence was broken by his mom's words: "Honey, let's go – we still need to check into our hotel and get unpacked!"

He couldn't wait to come back in the morning and for Saturday when he'd be standing next to Justin on his big day. However, just as he was starting to relax, he remembered he was going to miss the big game and felt a twinge of regret, wishing he could be with his team, too. Still, he had no doubt. He felt right about the decision he had made.

At the same time, he hoped they would be okay without him in the big game, now less than 40 hours away.

CHAPTER 11

THE BIG DAY

It was Saturday: Sarah and Justin's wedding day and the day of the big game. His mom was straightening his tie and getting herself ready for the ceremony. Ryan felt upbeat about being in Cape Cod with his family and participating in Sarah's special day. He pushed aside any thoughts that came into his mind about football.

"I'm really proud of you, Ryan, for making this decision on your own. I know it was hard, but I think you made the right decision," Ryan's mom said, smiling warmly at him.

Hearing his mother's words made him feel warm inside, and he smiled back. "Thanks, Mom."

"How did you end up deciding that Sarah's wedding was where you were meant to be?" she asked as she helped fold over his jacket collar.

"It was really hard to make this decision, but I thought about what it would feel like to miss the wedding and what it would feel like to miss the game. After Dad showed me how to ask myself good questions, and then find and evaluate my answers to take action on my decision, I imagined what both decisions would feel like. Deep inside, it just didn't feel right to miss the wedding. I couldn't do that to her. I just had to be here. Sarah is my favorite aunt. She's family," he replied with a twinkle in his eye.

"What you did, Ryan, was learn how to trust your gut instinct and follow your heart. I am so proud of you and so glad that you are here because I know Aunt Sarah would be really sad if you were not in the wedding," his mom said and gave him a big hug.

"I am glad I'm here, too," he said and felt a wave of happiness and satisfaction wash over him. It felt good to make a sacrifice for the sake of someone he loved. He thought about his team again and how they'd do without him, but felt they'd somehow find a way to get by. On the other hand, his aunt would have really missed him because he was her only nephew.

The wedding ceremony was beautiful, with unseasonably warm weather and spectacular puffy clouds that set a dramatic stage for this moment of a lifetime. Ryan stood next to Justin as his best man. Justin glowed with happiness as Sarah walked down the sandy aisle. She looked beautiful in her beach wedding dress. She had chosen to go with something flowing and airy. Her hair was loose and blew gently in the light autumn breeze. Sarah had specifically chosen a red and yellow rose bouquet because it was the colors of Ryan's team, the Tigers. Ryan smiled at this thoughtful touch and felt better by the minute.

After the ceremony, he sat at one of the tables, waiting for dinner to be served: it was going to be a surf and turf combo. Ryan was really excited at the thought of digging into his lobster. All of the guests were chatting, laughing, and enjoying the reception.

Ryan felt his phone vibrate in his pocket. It was a text from Jack: "end of first half…huge defensive battle…we're down 6-0."

Ryan felt a twinge of guilt and concern. *Would the score have been different if I was there?*

Sarah approached Ryan.

"Thank you so much, Ryan," she said, smiling. "I know this was a really hard decision for you and you had to make a big sacrifice. I want you to know that this day really wouldn't be the same without you." Sarah's eyes welled up with happy tears, which reminded Ryan how important he was to Sarah and confirmed, yet again, that he made the right decision. "I'm just so glad that you are here!"

"Me too, Aunt Sarah. It's been a really exciting and happy day! I wouldn't have wanted to miss it for anything."

Sarah patted Ryan on the shoulder and gave him a wink before she was whisked off to talk with the other guests. When Ryan turned back to the table, a big plate of food had arrived.

Losing track of time, he dove into his surf and turf. He then managed to convince the server to bring him another helping. Then, just as he was about to dive into his second lobster, he felt a buzz in his pocket. He pulled his phone out and saw that this time it was from Josh, the quarterback.

Ryan was very nervous. Maybe this was a text telling him that his team lost and blaming him for not being there. He held his breath, slowly drew his phone closer and tapped the screen. The text appeared:"we dug deep at the half…tigers 7, vikings 6…we won!!!"

PART 2

A Framework for Your Big Decisions
By Daniel Friedland, MD

CHAPTER 12

THE FOUNDATION FOR MAKING BETTER DECISIONS

As a father, it fills my heart with such joy to work on this project with my son, Zach. I love him with all my heart – always. But there is a memory I have when it feels like my heart wants to break open for him.

Zach was 10 years old when he first started playing Pop Warner football. He was so excited and busted his butt practicing five days a week, coming home each night those first couple of weeks with a wide-eyed smile, sharing his excitement of what had happened in practice. All until the night his coach assigned the boys their positions on the team... except for two young boys. Out of 24 kids, Zach was one of the two not assigned a position. That evening, he came home crushed, sobbing at what had happened.

Over the next week, he returned to practice. His smile was gone and he became all the more intense and determined to show the coach what he could do. One evening that week, I arrived to pick him up after practice, but I was a few minutes late.

As I crossed the field towards where he was standing near his coach, he caught my eyes. His eyes were filled with fury and he screamed at me, "Why are you so late!" In shock and anger, I responded, "You're lucky I pick you up at all!" As we crossed the field towards the car, I fumed, "Don't you ever talk to me like that in front of your coach again!"

Then something extraordinary happened. It still chokes me up to remember it. Zach and I were sitting at the traffic light on our way home. With a quiet voice he broke our stony silence, "Dad, I'm really sorry." This softened me a bit, but I was still not ready to let things go. I responded, "Why are you sorry?" awaiting his full penance. He responded, "I'm really angry at my coach, but I feel like I'm taking it out on you."

Every time I remember this moment, I can still feel how my heart completely melted. I was in awe of having been humbled by his emotional intelligence at the tender age of 10 years.

I feel this same sense of awe to be able to write this book with Zach now.

Now that Zach is becoming a young man, my deepest wish is for him to continue developing his emotional intelligence, especially his ability to make good decisions going forward in his life.

We began this project when Zach was in his 13th year. In the Jewish tradition, the age of 13 is a rite of passage into adulthood. Zach and I spoke about the importance of engaging in service of others as part of this rite. We discussed various options. A dear friend, Linda Sorkin, and her daughter, Skylar, had just finished writing a book, *Shining Through a Social Storm*, about teenage bullying. I asked Zach whether he would want to write a book with me to help young people like himself and adults make good decisions, especially big ones under challenging circumstances. I feel blessed that Zach agreed and that we can share this book with you.

Making good decisions is something that has been of great interest to me for over a decade. I'm a physician who wrote one of the early books on how all doctors are now trained to make medical decisions using a process called Evidence-Based Medicine. I've adapted this simple and powerful process I teach healthcare professionals and over the last three years have also been providing leaders with training programs and coaching on how to use this framework to make better decisions at work and at home.

In the first part of the book, Zach has written about how his protagonist, Ryan, went about using the framework his father gave him to make a difficult decision between playing in his big championship football final and going to his Aunt Sarah's wedding.

What I'd like to offer in this second part of the book is to go deeper in sharing how you too can use this Framework for making better life decisions, whether you are a teen like Zach or an adult also looking for new ways to make better decisions at home or at work.

If you are a teenager reading this section, it can be helpful to read and discuss this together with your parents or another adult you trust.

Alternatively, if you are a parent or a teacher reading this, you may also find it helpful to read it with your child or students, share thoughts and explore any questions that may arise.

Learning how to make good decisions is the key to taking wise action, which affects all aspects of your life. This includes the quality of your health and relationships, the fulfillment you find in the work you do or career you choose, and how happy and successful you will be.

Before we get into the Framework for making better decisions, let's set the foundation for making them.

This begins with a basic understanding of how your brain works. We'll talk about that first.

Then, once you understand how your brain works, you'll discover a scientifically proven method to better work your brain so you can think more clearly and be primed to decide.

Finally, you'll learn how to structure your thinking using a 4-Step Framework that will help you make better decisions – the very same Framework Ryan used to make his Big Decision.

So let's get started and explore some of the core basics about how your brain works.

CHAPTER 13

KNOW HOW YOUR BRAIN WORKS

Here's a brief user's guide on your brain. Knowing how your brain works will set you up to better work your brain in the next chapter, which will then prepare you to make better decisions in those that follow. Please know this overview oversimplifies the complexities of this powerful organ, much of which is not fully understood, and will likely never be. There's a saying: "If the brain were simple enough for us to understand, we'd be too simple to understand it!"

There are two key regions of your brain that play a major role in the decisions you make[1-6]:

1. The Limbic System is one of the most primitive parts of the brain. It operates *subconsciously* to engage your primal drives, including regulation of temperature, appetite, thirst, reproduction and sleep cycles.

It is also considered the seat of your emotional life. It includes an almond-shaped structure on each side of the brain called the amygdala, which is key to storing emotional memories of what feels good and bad and what's safe and dangerous. It also has dense connections to the pleasure center of the brain that plays an important role in the rewards we seek.

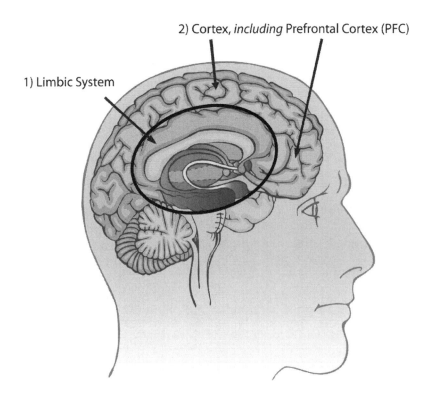

Your limbic system registers and remembers your likes and dislikes, compels you to seek short-term pleasure and protects you from danger. It's constantly scanning your environment and subconsciously registers whether it's "safe" or "unsafe." When it matches something as being "unsafe," it reflexively activates your threat circuitry and fight, flight or freeze responses to protect you from physical and psychological threats[7].

The limbic system evolved to help early humans "react" when they were threatened by attack from predators that lurked in the dangerous world they lived in. The limbic system enabled them to rapidly kick into high gear by speeding up their heart rate and breathing and pumping more blood to the extremities so they could either fight the animal or take flight by running away. And if neither of these responses were an option, they would freeze and play dead to protect themselves[7].

These days, many threats we feel are not based on physical survival. They're more emotional and psychological... the "what if" and all the bad outcomes we imagine might happen. We worry about being able to pay the mortgage, provide for our children, or failing any number of important tasks and how others might judge or reject us. Often these threats are based on our *perceptions* or *beliefs* rather than the reality of our circumstances.

Mark Twain said this best when he stated, "I've had a lot of worries in my life, most of which never happened."[8]

But even if the threat is psychological, like the fear of being excluded from your peers, your brain still reacts in the same way.

When your amygdala encounters a threat, whether it's physical or emotional, real or imagined, it triggers your fight and flight reactions. You subconsciously react to the threat by becoming "reactive," or what we call "going limbic."

In his classic books, *Emotional Intelligence* and *Social Intelligence*, Daniel Goleman refers to this being a "low road" brain process [1,2].

At first Ryan instinctively reacts to his dilemma along this low road. For Ryan, the conflict between choosing to play the championship game or go to his aunt's wedding first activated his limbic system, leading to a state of reactivity, in which he feels ambivalent, conflicted, stressed and fearful.

Behind his fear of letting his team and coach down, his deeper fear is that they would be so upset that they would reject him and he would feel disconnected and alone at school. Since his aunt is more understanding, he does not have this same fear of rejection with her. Thus, his limbic system is likely to tilt him toward playing for the team in the championship game to avoid feeling rejected.

The threat of rejection actually activates the same part of the limbic system where you suffer physical pain[9-12]. This is a big part of the reason why Ryan shares with his dad that this is a "painful decision for him."

This limbic threat explains why you may feel subconsciously compelled to make decisions to please others—a "fight" for validation—or alternatively avoid risky situations in which you might be rejected, like taking "flight" from public speaking, for example.

Ryan not only responds to the limbic threat of rejection. He is drawn to short-term pleasure, which is also connected to the limbic system. He's seduced by the thrill and intensity of the football championship, which can feel like the most important and exciting thing in the world and that nothing else matters.

As you can see, operating from the limbic system alone would cause humans to be highly impulsive decision makers. It exerts a powerful emotional force on your life, continually prompting you to react to internal perceptions and external circumstances, reflexively moving you away from perceived threats and towards immediate gratification.

But thankfully, you have another part of the brain that helps control your subconscious impulses and applies *conscious thinking* to those impulses and the decisions you make. It's your cortex, the outermost part located at the top of your brain.

2. The cortex is involved in *conscious awareness* and is responsible for complex processes such as impulse control, perception, planning, focus, shifting attention and more thoughtful decision making.

Daniel Goleman refers to cortical brain processing as the "high road." It is the key to conscious awareness, seeing the big picture, incorporating your values, considering others, formulating strategies, decision making, and implementing a well thought through plan[1-3].

The cortex is the part of the brain where you can become more proactive and *fully aware of the decisions you make.*

In contrast to the reactive limbic fight and flight response, Suzanne Segerstrom, a psychologist from the University of Kentucky, has coined a different term that characterizes how the cortex deals with internal conflict. She calls this the "Pause and Plan" response[13,14].

Unlike the limbic-driven fight and flight response that revs you up to take action automatically, the "Pause and Plan" response engages your cortex to slow down your physiology, including your heart rate and breathing, enabling you to take the time to consciously process your circumstances and decide what's best to do before you act[15].

There is one critical area of your cortex in particular that is largely responsible for coordinating your conscious awareness and ability to slow down, strategize and respond more effectively to make wise decisions. It's the prefrontal cortex (PFC), the front part of your brain behind your forehead.

The PFC is involved in a number of critical brain functions [4,5,15-17].

- With its connections to the amygdala, it can calm powerful emotions and enable you to pause before you act so you can avoid making rash, emotionally charged decisions and plan more effectively.

- It receives input from regions of your body, including your heart and gastrointestinal tract, enabling you to bring empathy and intuition ("gut instinct") to your decisions.

- It integrates circuits involved in social awareness and morality, so you can see things from another's perspective to bring your underlying values to the decisions you make.

- It enables short-term memory, where you can hold and weigh the information you bring to your decision.

- It includes the circuitry that is involved in executive functions, such as judgment, planning, prioritizing what's truly important and is critical for decision making itself.

- It is also the part of the brain that's crucial for

willpower—what you need to follow though and take action on your difficult decisions.

Robert Sapolsky, a professor and neuroscientist at Stanford University, has succinctly stated that the main purpose of the prefrontal cortex is to engage the brain "to do the harder thing."[15,18]

To be clear, your limbic system does not necessarily lead you astray in your decisions. In fact, this subconscious part of your brain is also regarded as being important to the decisions we make[17]. Often it provides the emotional fuel moving us towards or away from the action we need to take. For example, if your business is failing, the fear you experience can motivate you to make important decisions to take action and adjust your course. Or if someone is abusing you or a loved one, your anger can motivate your decision to be assertive and stop the abuse or get away from it.

But your limbic system is mostly focused on short-term threats and rewards, which can sometimes diverge from your longer-term goals and your values. To consciously and proactively make better decisions, you want your prefrontal cortex to be in the driver's seat, mindfully observing, regulating and integrating what your limbic system has to contribute.

In Ryan's case, if he only based his decision in the limbic part of his brain—the low road—he'd mainly be driven by the need to seek relief from the pain of social rejection or be seduced by the frenzy and pleasure of playing in the big game. He'd take the path of least resistance and do the easier thing. He'd play it safe by taking "flight" from feeling rejected, "fight" to maintain the approval of his teammates and coach and play for glory in the championship.

But his decision ends up coming from a different place: his cortex, or the "high road." Here he is able to find the strength and willpower to pause and come up with a plan that reflects his deeper values and priorities: the importance of family, how much his aunt and uncle-to-be truly mean to him, and a broader and longer-term view of wanting to honor these values and relationships.

He is able to engage his prefrontal cortex and regulate his limbic system to make a more conscious, well-thought-out decision, and do the harder thing that results in a better long term outcome.

Next, you'll learn about a key practice that enabled Ryan to better work his brain to do this and that can empower you to do so, too.

CHAPTER 14

KNOW HOW TO BETTER WORK YOUR BRAIN WITH MINDFULNESS

What's exciting is that more than a decade out from the "decade of the brain," astounding progress has been made in brain science. We now have brain imaging techniques, like functional MRIs, that detect where blood flows in the brain, as well as electroencephalograms that register brain wave activity, to illuminate the behaviors, skills and practices that can shift electrical activity and blood flow between various brain regions.

Research has shown how *you can actually learn how to shift activity in your brain from the subconscious limbic system to your prefrontal cortex*[19-24], *which is crucial to the decisions you make*[17]. If you learn the skills and practices to do this, you can leverage all the critical decision-making power that your brain has to offer.

Not only this, but scientists have discovered something that has changed everything we thought we knew about the brain.

When I went through medical school, I was taught that by

the age of five, you have all the brain cells (neurons) you're ever going to have and that individual parts of your brain, with their specific functions, are static and resistant to change. We were also taught that if your brain was damaged, by trauma or otherwise, it was unlikely to recover its functioning.

What we now know is that the brain can grow new neurons (a process called neurogenesis) and continually rewire and re-shape itself, not only in young developing brains, but through-out your life span...into your 80s and even your 90s! The brain is moldable or "plastic." Consequently, this process has been called "neuroplasticity."[25]

And here what's truly phenomenal and most encouraging. You have the power to rewire your own brain[26].

One of the most powerful ways to do this is through the thoughts you have. Just like working out in the gym to build muscle, certain ways of thinking can strengthen your brain, es-pecially the circuits in important areas of your cortex.

Rather than reacting to stressful circumstances from your limbic system, you can learn to more fully engage your pre-frontal cortex and rewire your brain to more effectively soothe your limbic system and think more clearly, creatively and proactively.

You can consciously build a more resilient brain to make better decisions under stressful circumstances.

You can learn to do this at any age... but what a blessing to be able to do it in your teen years, when the brain is still ac-tively developing.

So, what's the key to doing this?

By becoming more consciously aware and learning how to direct your attention.

Conscious awareness involves *noticing* the thoughts and feelings you're having in any given moment, and being able to take a more objective perspective on them by becoming an unbiased, non-judgmental, curious and caring observer.

This practice is known as mindfulness.

Mindfulness practice has been made widely available in the West through the work of John Kabat-Zinn, who founded the Mindfulness-Based Stress Reduction (MBSR) Program at The Center for Mindfulness at the University of Massachusetts Medical Center. It is now widely taught in academic and non-academic settings globally[27,28].

The practice has far-reaching health benefits (including for anxiety[29], relapse from depression[29], ADHD[30], eating disorders[31,32], addiction[32,33], irritable bowel syndrome[34-36], psoriasis[37], fibromyalgia[38-41], obesity[42,43] and pain[44-46]). It has also been scientifically proven to *calm the limbic system, shift activity in the brain to the prefrontal cortex and rewire the brain to become more focused and resilient in the face of stress*[24,47-49].

Mindfulness has been defined as the practice of paying attention, with a sense of curiosity, openness, kindness and non-judgmental acceptance of whatever is arising in the present moment[28].

It enables you to become more aware of your awareness itself and the stream of sensations, feelings and thoughts that flow through your conscious mind without over identifying or becoming entangled in your thoughts, sensations and feelings.

Ryan's Dad introduced him to the practice of mindfulness

by sharing how he pauses to observe his thoughts and feelings in his body without judging them when he begins to feel stressed. "Kind of like watching clouds move across the sky."

When you become more consciously aware, you are free to decide how best to act in light of your thoughts and feelings.

For example, instead of being swept away and reflexively reacting to stress-related feelings like anxiety, anger or fear, mindfulness enables you to recognize that you are not these thoughts and feelings. Rather than *being* anxious, angry or fearful you become aware that you are simply *having* anxious, angry or fearful thoughts and feelings. This opens a space in which you are able to pause before you act and take this time to decide and plan on the best possible action to take.

In addition to facilitating greater awareness, one of the core mindfulness practices helps you to direct and sustain your attention on anything you choose, such as your breath for example. Here the instructions would be to simply focus your attention on your breath, wherever you may notice it easily, such as the air moving in and out at the rim of your nostrils or the rise and fall of your belly. In this practice, it's common to also notice thoughts, sensations and feelings that pull your attention away from your area of focus—here, your breath.

The object of the practice is not to free your mind of these "distractions" but simply to notice them with a sense of curiosity, openness and kindness and then to gently and firmly bring your attention back to your breath, or whatever else you have chosen to focus on, over and over again.

This mindfulness practice builds the "muscle" or ability in your brain to be able to shift your attention at will and continually refocus it on whatever you choose. It builds pathways in your brain to strengthen your prefrontal cortex. This enables you to become more aware, more fully focus your attention, better regulate your limbic system and build willpower[15].

Mindfulness is important to the decisions you make because it enables you to calm your limbic system, see your thoughts more clearly and consciously, proactively seed new thoughts, and recognize those that align with your values and inspire you. It further enables you to weigh all of the insights you receive to better work your brain—to mindfully leverage your higher cortical thinking so you can make more inspired and better decisions. It also empowers you to build and leverage your willpower to follow through and take action on your decisions.

Knowing how your brain works and being able to mindfully work your brain sets a crucial foundation for making decisions.

The big question now is: How can you structure your thinking to make better decisions mindfully?

The following 4-Step Framework can help you. It's the framework that helped Ryan arrive at his big decision and is a process I've adapted from the way all doctors are now trained to make medical decisions.

CHAPTER 15

Introducing The 4-Step Framework for Making Better Decisions

I'd like to first share with you how I discovered that this framework can be applied to inspire life decisions. The discovery came to me during a very stressful and painful time in my life.

One evening in 2008, I hit bottom. I was consumed by stress and self-doubt, thinking I'd made a terrible decision in my life. I felt I'd become disconnected from my purpose and what inspires me the most, which ironically is helping others to navigate stress and self-doubt and make better life decisions by connecting with what inspires them the most.

I'd found this sense of purpose after I fell apart during my second year in medical school at the University of California, San Francisco, which caused me to appreciate just how overwhelming feelings of stress and self-doubt can be. As I wrestled with my insecurity, I felt intensely alone because all my medical school colleagues seemed so well-adjusted. To my astonishment, I learned from my counselor that more than half of the medical students in my class were getting counseling, too. But none of us had shared our struggles with each other, which left us all feeling alone.

Consequently, I formed the UCSF Medical Student Network, which ultimately enrolled every medical student into groups that provided them with emotional support. The Network provided us with an avenue to more openly discuss the stress and self-doubt we felt and to find ways to learn how to create meaning out of suffering. This enabled us to become more re-silient and compassionate healers and make better decisions to live a richer life.

Creating this network was one of the most meaningful and fulfilling things I've done. It connected me with my purpose in wanting to dedicate myself to this life work.

And here's where I initially thought I had taken a detour and had made bad decision.

After my medical residency, I was asked to become the first teaching fellow at UCSF. While I wanted to focus my fellow-ship on helping physicians and patients navigate stress and become more resilient, I was advised that this would not be a wise choice for my professional development and was steered into doing something "more academic."

As my second choice, I decided to train the faculty at UCSF on something that was just emerging in the scientific literature: Evidence-Based Medicine. This is a process that enables health-care providers to apply the best available scientific information to make better decisions and better care for their patients. It led to me authoring *Evidence-Based Medicine: A Framework for Clinical Practice*[50], one of the first textbooks on a topic that has become the standard by which all healthcare decisions are now made.

I then spent the next ten years teaching and training thousands of physicians and allied healthcare providers across the U.S. how to leverage scientific information to make better decisions and better care for their patients.

But I felt like I'd lost my way only teaching Evidence-Based Medicine. As the years passed by, I felt increasingly restless and disconnected from the heart of healthcare and from my source of inspiration and sense of purpose.

Ironically, I was filled with self-doubt because I thought I'd made a bad decision in narrowly focusing my path on helping physicians make good scientific-based decisions.

I yearned to feel inspired doing the work that's most meaningful to me, which is supporting others to connect with what inspires them the most to make better life decisions.

Fast-forward to the life-changing evening in 2008 when everything came to a head. Earlier in the day I'd taken my younger son, Dylan, for a walk on the trail down to Torrey Pines Beach. As he walked in front of me I followed, choking back tears, afraid he'd turn around and see me so sad. I also felt guilty that I was unable to enjoy this "idyllic" moment with my son in our spectacular surroundings. Later that evening after trying my best to focus on reading him a bedtime story, I lay in bed, restless and deeply troubled with thoughts and feelings of stress and self-doubt, compounded with the shame that they were getting in the way of me connecting with my son.

A torrent of painful thoughts swept me away—regrets over the career decision I'd made. How could I have taken this path to become an expert in Evidence-Based Medicine when every fiber of my being had wanted to help others navigate stress and make better decisions to live a more meaningful life? And here I was, desperately searching for a way to do this myself.

When we get stressed, we go limbic and our thoughts tend to focus on all of the bad things that could happen, the regrets of our past and what's wrong with us and others.

This fateful evening, the question, "What's wrong with me?" reverberated in my mind. My self-judgmental question tormented me, locking me down with inner tension. I felt disoriented and sick to my stomach, and all my muscles felt tense. The question had swept me away in a painful contortion of despair.

Then, something miraculous happened. Another question popped into my mind. One that I had never had before. I asked, "How can I find my way home?"

As I became consciously aware of this question, my body instantly released. I felt a sense of clarity and stillness that I don't think I would ever have found with years of therapy or drugs.

I was in total awe of what had just happened. Something had suddenly flipped my mind to a new way of thinking and had entirely changed the way I was viewing things.

I then realized that all I did was ask a better question. Instead of asking, "What's wrong with me?" I asked the question, "How can I find my way home?"

It then struck me that what I had been doing the last decade was teaching doctors how to ask better questions through teaching Evidence-Based Medicine (EBM).

I had been teaching doctors the following 4-step scientific decision-making process that begins by empowering healthcare providers to 1) **Frame** the right questions to begin with.

It then proceeds to help them 2) **Find** the best available scientific research to answer these questions in computer databases and then 3) **Evaluate** and 4) **Apply** the research to make the best possible healthcare decision with their patients[51,52].

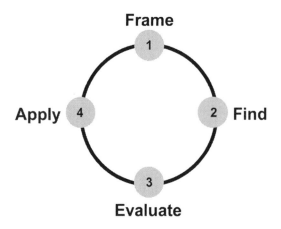

I then saw the congruence and meaning in my journey—and that EBM was not the detour as I had initially thought. Rather it was the path I was meant to travel.

What I discovered is that in addition to helping make scientific-based medical decisions, the framework of EBM can help you make more inspired life decisions as well!

The framework that doctors use to make better medical decisions can be applied to making all of your important decisions, whether you make them at home or at work.

I've adapted the EBM Framework to incorporate what you've learned earlier about mindfulness and how your brain works to empower you to make better life decisions by engaging the following 4 steps to:

1. **Frame** more inspired questions;
2. **Find** more inspired answers by optimizing your brain;
3. **Evaluate** whether your answers and decision truly feel "right"; and
4. **Apply** your decision by taking purposeful action in your life.

Let's take a deeper look at this Framework, step-by-step, and see how Ryan was able to leverage it to mindfully work his brain to make his big decision.

We'll first begin with how you can learn to *Frame* the right questions in making a difficult decision.

CHAPTER 16

STEP 1: FRAME YOUR QUESTIONS

The quality of the answers you receive or insights you have is very much dependent on the quality of the questions you frame.

Under stress, your limbic system subconsciously influences the type of thoughts and questions that run through your mind. This part of your brain is built to respond to threats in one of three ways: fight, flight, or freeze[7].

Initially when Ryan was going limbic, his thoughts and the types of questions he asked tilted in this way, reflecting each of these responses to stress:

1. **Fight**: Here he initially got angry and looked for someone else to blame, thinking, *How could my aunt Sarah do this? How could she not know the wedding could land on the day of the championship final and not plan this better?*

2. **Flight**: This is the type of thinking that's related to us wanting to run away from what threatens us. It's reflected in Ryan, when he turns his thoughts to the question, *How can I get out of this?* Looking for the easy way

out, he begins to fantasize about escaping his predicament by telling his aunt that his coach is forcing him to
play or telling his coach that his parents are forcing him
to go to the wedding.

3. **Freeze**: When an animal gets completely overwhelmed
with a threat, it may become immobilized or even play
dead. Just before speaking to his father, Ryan became so
overwhelmed and anxious by the stress of his decision
that he froze, wanting to give up. He silently hoped that
his parents would make the decision for him.

Some would say that this type of thinking reflects a "victim" mindset to escape responsibility. Judgment aside, this
simply reflects how the limbic system automatically responds
under stress. It's how the brain developed to keep us safe.

As noted above, the limbic system developed relatively early in our evolution. So, it also has a very strong gravitational
pull and is very influential in the way we are all predisposed
to think.

In addition, the limbic system is subconscious. It's the "low
road" that sits below your "high-road" cortex, which is the seat
of your conscious awareness. This mindset is the path of least
resistance that many of us fall into reflexively, without even
knowing it.

When better decision-making skills are called for, you can
learn how to elevate your thinking to avoid "low-road" or limbic brain processing and consciously shift your thinking into
your higher-road cortical circuits.

Just as my mind flipped that life-changing evening to my
higher-road circuits with the question "How can I find my way

home?" from my low-road rumination over "What's wrong with me?" learning how to consciously frame more inspired questions shifts your thinking, too. It activates and reinforces higher-level circuits in your brain, leading to different types of answers, actions and results.

Making the shift to more consciously *frame better questions* begins with mindful awareness of all the thoughts and questions—your internal dialogue—that tend to stream through your mind. For example, next time you're feeling stress, just try to notice your thoughts, without judging them. Do they involve all the bad things that could happen or questions like "what's wrong with me" or "what's wrong with others?"

As we've mentioned, research suggests that mindfulness and recognizing reactive thoughts and emotions are key to helping you activate your prefrontal cortex and deactivate your amygdala to take the edge off your reactivity so you can think more clearly and productively[19-22].

Remember that mindfulness is the ability to take a third-person perspective on the thoughts you are having. It is the practice of paying attention non-judgmentally with a sense of openness, curiosity, and compassion for whatever is arising in the present moment.

It's important to meet whatever thoughts you are having, particularly those that are stress-related, with a spirit of understanding and kindness, just as Ryan's dad showed him compassion for the struggles he was having.

Had Ryan's father snapped at him, "Stop blaming others! You need to take responsibility!" or had Ryan gotten down on himself in much the same way, this would have further activated the threat circuitry in his limbic system and escalated his anxiety and stress. This in turn would have drawn mental resources away from his higher cortical circuits and limited Ryan's ability to think flexibly and creatively.

In fact, when you go limbic, not only do you tend to be less *responsible*, but you are less *response-able*. That's because you cannot easily access your prefrontal cortex to make better decisions. Your limbic system is in control. You are more likely to get swept away in a narrow range of well-grooved fight and flight responses that are primarily designed to protect you from harm.

Mindful awareness, with its qualities of kindness and compassion for yourself, cultivates a sense of safety. This enables you to transfer activity from your fear-based limbic system to your higher cortical circuits. Those cortical circuits allow you to apply more highly developed skills like focusing on your values and seeing the bigger picture so you can respond more adaptively with a wider range of options.

Another quality of mindfulness that helps you frame higher quality questions is curiosity. This quality inspires you to explore, discover and grow. It transforms your decisions into puzzles, from limbic-activating problems to be survived to prefrontal cortical challenges to be solved.

The moment you become mindfully aware of your stress-related and automatically patterned thoughts, you are primed and ready to proactively re-seed your internal dialogue and further engage your "high-road" circuits with more inspired and productively framed questions.

To set your intention to frame good questions simply start

with the question, "What are the good questions I can ask?"

While this is a personal journey and each person may ask different questions, here are some more specific questions that can help to inspire your own in making better decisions under challenging circumstances:

- What are all of the alternatives?
- What are all of the possible outcomes, not only in the short term but the long term, too?
- Who are the people that are most important to me, and how will this decision affect them?
- What are my most important values?
- What are my most important goals?
- What decision is most aligned with my values and goals?
- What will I decide to do?

Ryan's dad seeds some of these questions for him when he says, "Ryan, it can help to make sure you've thought of all the possible options and the likely consequences of each option not only in the short term, but how this will affect your life in the long term. Also, think about the people involved and what feels most important to you in your life. Ultimately, you have to make a decision that feels right and that you can live with."

These are some of the questions that Ryan worked through to ensure that his decision aligned with his deepest values and priorities.

Ryan first tried to consider all his alternatives, including playing the game and then heading out to the wedding, but the timing didn't work. He briefly considered asking his aunt to change the date of the wedding, but quickly realized that this had already taken an immense amount of planning, and asking to change it felt selfish and unreasonable.

Sometimes decisions are not an "either...or..." They are an "and." Some of the best solutions at the outset result from thinking creatively around coming up with options that somehow include both alternatives. However, this did not help Ryan. In his situation, either going to the wedding or playing the championship game were the only options for him to consider.

Ryan then went on to ask himself about the possible outcomes of each of these options. He also considered who were the people involved and how would it affect each of them, as well as what he was valuing the most in considering each option.

The questions I've shared above and those that Ryan asked himself are not intended to be prescriptive, or that these would be the only questions you would ask under similar circumstances. Rather, they are intended to inspire you to consider questions like these, in addition to the questions that would be helpful to your specific situation.

Can you think of any other questions it would have been helpful for Ryan to ask?

After framing good questions, you are off to a good start in making your decision. The next part of the process focuses on creating an optimal brain state to best *Find* the answers to your questions.

CHAPTER 17

STEP 2: FIND YOUR ANSWERS

When Ryan first approached his father to find answers to his dilemma, his dad saw that Ryan was upset—that he was "going limbic."

As we discussed above, it's difficult to make good decisions in a limbic or reactive state of mind, because you don't have full access to your higher circuits of thinking, including your prefrontal cortex, which is crucial for making conscious and well-considered decisions.

When you feel stressed around your decisions, it's important to find a way to soothe your limbic system and open up your higher cortical circuits so the answers to your questions can best find you.

Ryan's dad helps him do this by asking Ryan what activity or setting he finds most effective to calm himself down. Ryan responds that whenever he gets mad or frustrated, he finds it helpful to take a walk, go for a run or lie on his bed quietly in his room to calm down.

His dad then went on to share another way he taught his

patients and that he used himself to calm down. Breathing mindfully!

He explained, "All I do is just get into a quiet place, then simply watch my thoughts and feelings in my body without judging them. Kind of like watching clouds move across the sky. And then I just bring my attention to my breathing and breathe in a slow and relaxed way."

He then instructed Ryan to breathe in slowly over about 5 seconds and out slowly over 5 seconds or so. And to breathe with a "soft belly," noticing how it expands as he breathes in and recedes as he breathes out.

His father then explained why breathing mindfully helps you think more clearly so you can make more effective decisions.

When you breathe mindfully, you are activating the parasympathetic part of your nervous system (PNS). The PNS counterbalances the sympathetic nervous system (SNS), which revs you up, increasing your heart and breathing and redistributing blood from your gut and growth-oriented *rest* and *digest* functions to prepare for *fight* and *flight* limbic responses[7,53].

In contrast to your SNS, your PNS helps to soothe your limbic system, slowing down your breathing and heart rate and returning blood to your rest and digest functions. It's this part of your nervous system that enables you to calm down and think more clearly so you can *pause* and *plan* to make more effective decisions[14,15].

One of the largest PNS nerves in the body is the vagus nerve, running from your brain stem and branching off to stimulate major internal organs, such as your heart, gut, and lungs. It also stimulates contraction of the diaphragm. And this is where you can take control of your body and consciously calm yourself down.

When you breathe in and out with a full and relaxed excursion of the diaphragm (i.e., with a "soft belly"), you can increase activity in the PNS, which naturally counterbalances and decreases activity in your amygdala and SNS that drive your limbic stress responses.

You can also intensify the calming effect of your "soft belly" breathing by breathing out with a more prolonged exhalation like you are breathing out slowly through a straw (e.g., breathing in for a five-second count and breathing out for an eight-second count)[54]. Try experimenting with this to see how you feel.

At the same time, breathing mindfully this way this promotes activity in your higher cortical circuits which enables you to think more consciously and clearly so you can find better answers to make better decisions.

The quality of mindfulness that can help you to find your answers is that of openness. By learning how to soothe his limbic system through mindful breathing, Ryan allowed his body and brain to become receptive and become more aware of whatever was arising in him.

This gave him a greater sense of peace and clarity of mind. In other words, through his father's guidance, Ryan was encouraged to create the optimal conditions to access his higher cortical circuits where he could more freely receive and *find* the answers to his questions.

As Ryan did his soft belly breathing, he calmed down and began to see things more clearly. He could see the ramifications of each decision. He was able to find the answers to all of the questions he'd asked himself.

When he thought about going to the wedding, he envisioned the disappointment of his coach and teammates. He imagined how they'd be angry that he let them down and how this could also jeopardize his ability to play for the team the following year.

He was also able to notice that these thoughts spiked his anxiety and his body became tense. So for good measure, he took a few more soft belly breaths to calm himself down and continue.

He then saw how, if he played in the football game, his Aunt Sarah, Justin, and his parents would be disappointed, even if they said they'd understand. He could also see that they wouldn't be at the game to cheer him on, which was part of what made the games so much fun for him.

When Ryan asked himself who was most important to him, he was aware of his loyalty to his coach and team, but was equally aware that his Aunt Sarah was family, had always been there for him and would be there for him his whole life. He realized how much he loved her and Justin.

And then he realized what was truly important. It was what his parents had instilled in him over and over as a child and had become one of his core values. "There is nothing as important as family" was a family credo. He felt this deeply in his heart. While he loved football, he knew he probably wouldn't end up playing in college—it wasn't really his goal. Besides, there was still a possibility that he could play for the team next year.

But loyalty and being committed to his team were also

values that were important to him. He had to weigh this against what most mattered to him: family, especially since they would be with him for the long term.

With all of this to consider, Ryan begins to lean in the direction of going to the wedding, but how can he know it's ultimately the right decision for him? And after you find your answers to the questions you've framed and tilt towards your decision, how can you know it's the right decision for you, too? Here's where you get to *Evaluate* your answers and decision next.

CHAPTER 18

STEP 3: EVALUATE YOUR ANSWERS

Ryan actually tilted both ways before making his ultimate decision. He first leaned towards playing the championship game and felt a wave of relief doing so. But then later this feeling was replaced by a gnawing sense of restlessness and a wave of nausea. This decision did not feel right.

He then tilted towards going to the wedding, and his anxiety came back, but his heart and gut told him that this was the right decision. While this choice did not fully resolve his fear and conflict, he knew more deeply that this was the right answer to what he needed to do.

So the big question here is: How do you evaluate your answers and ultimate decision? A number of questions that serve as litmus tests can be very helpful to guide your decision here.

As you begin to evaluate your decision, ask yourself: *Does the decision feel right more than it feels good?*

This is not merely a matter of semantics. It relates to the part of your brain that is driving your decision.

Generally, when you do things because it feels "good," it is limbic-based. You are either experiencing the sweet relief of avoiding something painful or the reward of something that brings you pleasure.

On the other hand, doing something because it feels "right" relates more to your higher cortical circuits. It relates to a sense of congruence with your values, goals, morality and conscience.

These low-road and high-road circuits also take a different perspective with respect to time. The limbic system, which is partly designed to protect and keep you safe, tends to take an immediate view of things. From a limbic point of view, we want to feel good right now.

In contrast, your prefrontal cortex can envision the future. It's able to consider not only whether your decision feels good right now, but whether it would be right for you in the long term, too.

As we've discussed before, this is not to say that limbic-driven decisions are never good ones. We cannot argue with millions of years of evolution, where the limbic system has done a great job of protecting us from harm. We make many decisions to avoid doing things because they're potentially dangerous and don't feel good. In addition, the limbic system also draws us towards things that are good for us. For example, it drives emotional attraction and pair bonding, such as falling in love, which contributes to the richness of our lives.

But sometimes the limbic system can lead you astray if you base your decisions only on what feels good right now.

Ryan's mother shared the example of eating candy. She cautioned that while eating candy can feel really good in the short term, if you eat too much, it can make you feel sick. And it's definitely not healthy in the long term.

Likewise, doing other things like having risky sex, taking drugs or abusing alcohol can feel good in the moment, but can hurt you and others in the long term.

By calibrating yourself around whether your decisions feel "right," you can be guided by how your decisions express your higher-level cortical thinking and values and what will ultimately be good for you in the long term.

Mindfulness can be very helpful here too, particularly with its quality of discernment. This quality, as opposed to judging, enables you to see something more clearly and objectively, and sense how it adds to or detracts from the quality of your life.

You may also experience the sense of rightness as a deep knowing. Like when you have a sense of what feels right in your heart and gut. This is called "gut instinct" or "intuition."

Did you know that you have a rich collection of nerve networks in your gut and heart? Some have even referred to the gut as a "peripheral brain" or your "second brain."[55]

Signals from the heart and gut travel through a dense highway of fibers through a part of the brain called the insula[4]. When these signals integrate with the prefrontal cortex, it can register as either dissonance or a sense of rightness about a decision.

When Ryan ultimately makes his decision to go to the wedding, he knows that his decision feels right, not only in his brain, but in his heart and gut, as well. He noticed how his gut "untwisted" and how he felt in his heart that going to the wedding was the right choice for him.

In addition to this intuitive form of evaluating his decision, Ryan could also have taken a more analytical approach. For example, he could have made a list of the pros and cons to more explicitly weigh the merits of each decision.

This type of decision making leverages the prefrontal cortex[4,5]. Ryan would have to be in a relatively relaxed, yet focused state—that is, not going limbic—in order to apply such analytical decision-making skills. If you are going limbic, this type of analytical approach is likely to fail because your limbic system can hijack your prefrontal cortex—something Goleman calls "amygdala hijack."[2]

Once you have made your decision and it feels right, you can take heart that even if it feels daunting in the short term, it may well feel good on a sustainable basis over the long term.

Also, since your cortex integrates circuits of empathy, compassion, social awareness and morality, you are more able to reflect on whether your decision is not only right for you but how it impacts others, too. While you may not be able to please everyone, this helps you to stay mindful to communicate your decisions with empathy, compassion and respect.

Finally, your cortex is critical to planning and following through on what comes next: taking action to skillfully *Apply* your decision.

CHAPTER 19

Step 4: Apply Your Decision

Applying your decisions under challenging circumstances takes courage and willpower, particularly when you anticipate fallout, such as others getting upset or rejecting you. So even when you know from your cortex what you need to do to align with your higher values, your limbic system, ever vigilant for threats, may still leave you feeling apprehensive or scared.

Mindfulness enables you to take a third-person perspective to appreciate the tug between your values and fears, and pro-actively find the will and courage to take action to apply your decision under the most challenging of circumstances. The quality of mindfulness that helps here is steadfastness. This is cultivated by the commitment to direct and sustain your attention on a chosen object of focus (such as your breath, for example) in mindfulness practice.

Courage and steadfastness are not the absence of fear. Rather, they are the ability to find the strength and steadiness to stay the course and follow through on your values-based decision in spite of it.

The consequence of inaction because of fear may bring initial relief, but the incongruence of not following through on something you value will likely eat at you, leaving you feeling restless and unfulfilled.

While Ryan may have experienced a sense of rightness about his decision, he also experienced his anxiety, the product of an activated limbic system that had been triggered by his fear of rejection. He may have had the sense that his decision was the right one for him to make, but he still felt anxious about sharing his decision with his team. After all, even when your higher cortical circuits know what's right, your low-road limbic system still has a mind of its own.

Doing what you know feels right in the face of fear takes courage and willpower, which involves the ability to activate your prefrontal cortex to both calm and override your limbic system.

This is not easy for Ryan to do, let alone any adult, especially since at the tender age of 13, his higher cortical circuits and his prefrontal cortex will not be fully developed until he turns 25.

Furthermore, when fear sets in and the limbic system gets activated, it can draw resources away from the prefrontal cortex and your circuits of willpower. The prefrontal cortex is a more recent development in evolution; it's no match for a strongly activated limbic system and can fatigue.

Research on willpower has shown that when individuals expend mental energy regulating their limbic system with their prefrontal cortex, such as denying their feelings or desire to eat sugary snacks, their willpower fatigues and they have difficulty following through on tasks.

For example, in an experiment by Roy Baumeister, one of the leading researchers on willpower, some hungry individuals were instructed to eat only radishes while they were faced with having to resist the tempting sight and aroma of chocolate. These individuals were compared to a lucky control group who were instructed to eat the chocolate and not the radishes. The two groups were then assigned to solve an insoluble puzzle—a test of perseverance and willpower. Those who had spent their mental energy resisting chocolate quit working on the puzzles in less than half the time compared to the chocolate group[56].

In another experiment, 60 undergraduate psychology students from Case Western Reserve University were assigned to watch a disturbing 3-minute excerpt of the documentary *Mondo Cane*, which discusses environmental disasters (involving radioactive waste) on wildlife. The movie showed heart-wrenching scenes of sick and dying animals. One group of students was instructed to be stoic and not show any emotion. Another that served as a control group got to watch the movie normally and freely express whatever they felt. Both groups were then tested on their ability to persist in squeezing a hand exerciser, a measure of willpower. The stoic group who'd spent their mental energy suppressing their emotional reactions quit much sooner. Their willpower had been depleted[57].

The theory is that with intense or prolonged use of the prefrontal cortex, glucose and activity in this part of your brain begins to diminish, which undermines your willpower and ability to continue regulating your limbic system[15,58].

This explains why coming home from work before you've had dinner can be a treacherous time for you and your family. When you've been making decisions all day and are feeling tired and hungry, you tend to be more on edge, so little things can irritate you. At the same time, your prefrontal cortex does not have the resources to regulate your limbic activity to prevent you from responding in ways that you later regret.

You need to optimize your prefrontal cortex so that you can fully harness your willpower to take action in the face of fear. This is why Ryan's father advised him to make sure he got a good night's sleep and was well nourished and hydrated before he spoke with his team. Ryan was also prepared to breathe mindfully to maintain the activity in his prefrontal cortex.

In addition to the strength he found internally, Ryan also found external support from the people he trusted most to help him be accountable for taking his chosen action. In Ryan's case, he was grateful for the support he received from his Aunt Sarah, who deeply appreciated how difficult it was for him to face his coach and teammates. He also deeply appreciated the fact that his parents would support him no matter what.

And so, leveraging his internal and external resources, Ryan is able to recognize his fear, but rather than fighting or taking flight from it, he finds the strength and willpower to take the action that is aligned with his deepest values in the face of his fear. Even though he was anxious to face his team, he summoned his courage to persevere and face his teammates and coach.

Ryan's father also advised him to practice in his mind what he was going to do before he took action. Another key element in skillfully applying your decision is the specific way you communicate and execute it.

Rehearsing in your mind what you will say and how you act can be very helpful to prepare for the pivotal moment when you express your decision with others, particularly those it might affect unfavorably.

Part of the reason why this is important is that in the heat of the moment, you can easily be swamped by your limbic responses and express yourself in ways you might later regret. For example, under stress you might fall into the trap of justifying yourself, acting like a victim or disrespecting the feelings of others.

Preparing for this challenging moment helps you remain steadfast in expressing yourself authentically and clearly. This yields the greatest likelihood that while others may not agree with your decision, they will still respect you for it. This not only has the potential to preserve your relationships, but may deepen it with others, too.

Ryan rehearsed his big moment, playing out in his mind over and over how he'd talk to his coach and teammates. He was able to recognize his nervous reaction and practice his soft belly breathing to calm himself down. Calming himself this way seemed easier and more effective each time he rehearsed this. He also practiced speaking slowly and clearly and thought through what he wanted to say, and he envisioned the outcome he was hoping to achieve in the interaction.

And so, when the time came, he was prepared. It played out much the way he'd imagined and rehearsed it—perhaps even better.

In that delicate moment when he shared his decision with his coach and teammates, he registered their shock and disappointment, which brought up feelings of anxiety. But he was able anticipate and mindfully observe these feelings. Rather than being swept away and retreating, he was able to breathe through this stress, stand up straight, make eye contact, offer a sincere apology and clearly express his choice to go to his aunt's wedding.

The demeanor with which he was able to stay present, grounded and steadfast in his decision began to turn the tide of sentiment on the field. Shock and disappointment turned to empathy and understanding, and ultimately respect. Ryan had successfully applied his decision.

You've now completed the four steps in this Frame-Find-Evaluate-Apply Decision-Making Framework. But you're not done yet. After Applying your decision, you come full circle. Looping back to Step 1, you again *Frame* your key questions....

CHAPTER 20

STEP 1: FRAME YOUR QUESTIONS AGAIN

After taking action to Apply your decisions, you circle back to Step 1, and again Frame questions, such as, "Did I make the right decision?" or "Was my decision aligned with my values?" or "Is there anything else I now need to do?"

After all was said and done, Ryan reflected on his decision. He realized that he had made one of the most difficult decisions of his life, and he felt secure that he'd done the right thing. Rather than just feeling good in the short term, he experienced a more sustained sense of well-being that came from knowing that he'd done the right thing. He was aligned to what he valued most, and he felt complete with his coach and team and connected with his family, Aunt Sarah, and Justin, his new uncle.

Moreover, he felt stronger than ever before. He had discovered a newfound confidence that he could face anything. He now knew that he could make good decisions under challenging circumstances.

CHAPTER 21

IN SUMMARY

We can celebrate that Ryan made a decision that was right for him. However, this story was not about the decision itself being universally right—that it's always right to go to an important family function over a team-based sporting event. Rather, it's about how you can arrive at your own best decision using the 4-Step Framework:

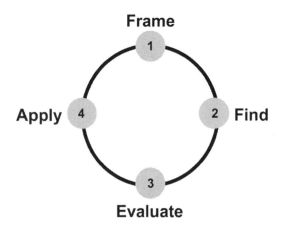

You've learned how the framework helps you to:

1. *Frame* your questions;
2. *Find* your answers;
3. *Evaluate* your answers and decision; and take action to
4. *Apply* your decision.

The ultimate decision you make is dependent on your unique situation, values, goals, and priorities that you hold.

Ryan may have made a different decision had his circumstances been different. For example, what if this has been the final year of high school and his dream had been to play college football, and some of the top college football scouts were going to be at the championship game? Would this have changed his decision?

Or what if you were a professional athlete, which enabled you to provide for your spouse and children? Would you be able to make the choice to go to an important family function instead of playing in the big game?

Decisions are made in a particular context. This 4-Step Framework empowers your decisions within your specific context.

The process of using these 4 steps in the Framework is also highly dynamic. While your decisions may loop around in the Frame-Find-Evaluate-Apply sequence, as you begin to use this process you may notice these steps may also oscillate between each other.

For example, you may frame your questions and find your answers that lead to new questions and answers. You may then evaluate your answers that converge on a decision that you then evaluate further. This leads to the application of your decision, which then leads to new questions in which you evaluate whether the action you took worked.

The sequence of steps with which you begin this decision making process may also be modified. For example, if you feel so stressed about your decision that you can't think clearly enough to frame your inspired questions, you may want to flip Step 1 and Step 2 by first finding an optimal brain state to become more receptive before you frame your questions.

In this situation, first finding a way to calm your limbic system, like going out for a run, taking a warm shower or engaging in soft belly breathing, may be the best place to start to help you find sufficient mental clarity to begin framing your questions next.

In this Find-Frame-Find... sequence, you can then continue to mindfully engage in the activities that facilitate an optimal brain state so that the answers to your questions can best find you.

Rather than being constrained by a specific sequence, what's important is to use each of the four steps and be fluid in sequencing them to arrive at your best possible decisions.

What you now have in your hands is a framework for engaging your brain to make better decisions. There's another benefit built into this process. It hinges on what we shared earlier about how your brain is "plastic."

Your brain has the capacity to rewire itself in neuroplastic transformation. Every time you engage in this process, you are not only making a better decision, but you are also hardwiring and consolidating the framework of related circuitry for making better decisions. So you not only get to make a good decision today, but you are also continually enhancing your ability to make more effective decisions tomorrow.

CHAPTER 22

In Conclusion

This 4-Step Framework for making better decisions is built on the foundation of mindfulness. It's a mindfulness-based Framework for making inspired decisions.

Mindfulness enables you to notice your conflicting thoughts, sensations and feelings without being swept away by a tsunami of stress. It enables you to consciously work your brain and engage in these 4 steps with a sense of curiosity, openness, discernment, and steadfastness to take courageous action.

There is another quality of mindfulness I'd like to conclude with. It's appreciation.

Appreciate the challenges of making good decisions under difficult circumstances. Appreciate the remarkable capacity of your brain to make inspired decisions in alignment with your deepest values. And appreciate yourself for wanting to learn how your brain works so you can more consciously work your brain to make better decisions. This is the groundwork of social, emotional and spiritual intelligence.

I deeply appreciate the opportunity to write this book with

Zach and to share this Framework for making better decisions with you.

My wish for Zach, my other son Dylan, and for you, is: May you Frame good questions, and Find, Evaluate and Apply your answers to make better decisions in your life for the benefit of all.

If you'd like to learn more about this Framework and find and give support to others in making better decisions, please join us at TheBigDecisionBook.com

About the Author:

ZACH FRIEDLAND

Iwas born in Berkeley, California, and currently live in San Diego, California, where I am in 8th grade. I play football and lacrosse, but my favorite sport is lacrosse. When I'm not busy with school, I also like to surf, skateboard and hang out with friends.

I chose to write this book to help others by offering a way to make decisions based on what feels right, rather than what feels good. I wanted to give people the tools to make better decisions so they can learn a new and possibly better way of doing things, feel more confidence and satisfaction from their decisions and better shape their lives. I am at the point in my life where I am starting to become more and more independent so I have to learn how to make good decisions in my life. In my journey of writing this book with my dad, I am learning how to make better decisions.

My dad brought me this opportunity as a "gift." I embraced it as my rite of passage into adulthood. Even though it was a great experience, it was also very time consuming to finish writing the book, causing me to miss out on some after school fun, weekends and even holidays. But I did it because I knew how much it could help you and me in our lives ahead of us.

I also learned a lot about the process of writing a book. Specifically, I discovered that you have to work hard, sometimes take a break and not force things, be *very* patient, breathe, ask the right questions, and let the answers come to you. I also learned that you sometimes have to rewrite and rework things many times before your project is complete. I realized that if you set your mind to do something, you can do it. And finally, just like when I felt most inspired playing football for my Torrey Pines Pop Warner team, I learned that the results you get from your efforts are directly proportional to what you put into something. If you can give it all you've got, even though it might be painful in the short term, it is worth it in the long run.

I found much of my inspiration from my dad who helped me develop the ideas in the book and taught me the responsibilities of leadership, teaching and helping others to guide them in living a meaningful life. My dad inspires me every day by working very hard and showing me that if you work hard on something, then it can be accomplished.

Also, my mom, Sue, inspires me everyday to work hard and helped me a lot in writing the book, giving me direction and editing this book. She takes on a lot everyday in taking care of our family and running our family business.

Last, I am greatly inspired by my brother Dylan, who is with me, by my side, everyday and will always be there for me, as I will be for him, now and in our future.

About the Author:

DANIEL FRIEDLAND, MD

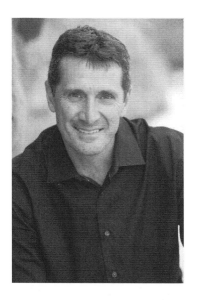

For more than a decade, Dr. Daniel Friedland has devoted himself to transforming the lives of leaders and their organizations, as well as healthcare providers and patients, with keynote addresses, workshops, coaching and online programs that integrate brain science, mindfulness and evidence-based medicine to:

- Effectively navigate stress;
- Make smarter health, business and life decisions;
- Optimize health, relationships and productivity; and
- Achieve peak performance.

He has worked with organizations such as GlaxoSmithKline, The Kaiser Permanente Federation, Blue Cross, Group Health, The Foundation for Medical Excellence, the US Army, Navy, and Air Force, Fairmont Raffles Hotels International, The YMCA, Conscious Capitalism, and Vistage – having delivered over 1500 programs, reaching more than 50,000 health care and business professionals nationally.

Board Certified in Internal Medicine, Dr. Friedland is the author of *"Evidence-Based Medicine: A Framework for Clinical Practice,"* one of the first textbooks to guide physicians in making effective medical decisions – now all physicians are trained this way.

Inspired with a purpose to help people navigate stress and focus on what's truly important in their lives, he has discovered how the framework of evidence-based medicine not only promotes scientific intelligence but also cultivates social, emotional and spiritual intelligence to empower conscious leadership, better life and work decisions and the health and well-being of individuals and organizations.

Dr. Friedland serves as Medical Director for Barney & Barney (a leading insurance brokerage), President-Elect of the American Board of Integrative Holistic Medicine, and President and CEO of SuperSmartHealth, which provides Seminars, Consulting, Coaching, and Executive Leadership and Wellness Programs, including the 8-week online program:

The 4 in 4 Framework™ to Achieve Peak Performance.

This program incorporates the Frame-Find-Evaluate-Apply framework outlined in The Big Decision to further empower you to navigate stress and optimize your health, relationships and productivity at home and at work.

For more information about "Dr. Danny" and the programs, resources and services he provides see DanielFriedland.com.

Zach's Acknowledgements

I would like to thank everyone that contributed to this book, who encouraged and inspired me and reviewed and edited countless versions.

In particular, I'd like to thank my 6th grade teacher, Erica Rood, who helped guide me through the beginning of the writing process and edited the early version of my section of this book. In addition, many thanks to my former 5th grade teacher, Lisa Wilken, for inviting me to return and partner with her to introduce my book and share it's lessons with her class.

I am deeply grateful to my football coaches, especially Roger Bingham, Duane Bickett, Paul Driscoll and Jeff Fargo, who encouraged me and had the confidence in me to allow me to run a lot of the big plays for my team.

I also want to thank my little brother Dyl, who gives me a reason to be a good example, and my mom, Sue Friedland, who spent countless hours helping me in the writing process, edited my book and generally provided support that only a mom can provide.

And finally, I'd like to thank my dad, Daniel Friedland, who made me see that anything is possible, if you just frame the right questions and allow yourself to find, evaluate and apply the right answers.

DANIEL'S ACKNOWLEDGEMENTS

I'd like to start by thanking Skylar Sorkin, Linda Sorkin and Colleen Ster, who inspired the idea for Zach and me to work together on this book.

I too would also like to thank Erica Rood and everyone who contributed to this book. Thanks to Colleen Morgans, a talented family portrait photographer and parent of one of Zach's football teammates, who became our team photographer. She graciously gave permission to use the action shots and headshot of Zach in his bio. Thanks to Robert Goold for my headshot and to Linda Sorkin for taking the wonderful picture of Zach and me at the back of the book. Thanks to Mike Perrone, our team videographer, who recorded, edited and allowed us to use the videos you see on our website. Thanks to Craig Gillis for suggesting a key edit and his support and friendship. And thanks to Damon for the "awesome" book cover as advertised (see damonza.com) and to Benjamin Carrancho for his keen eye in formatting the book.

Thanks also to Lisa Wilken, Zach's former 5th grade teacher, for inviting him to share his book with her class and directly experience how its lessons can make a difference in young lives.

I am grateful to the pioneering work of the Evidence-Based Medicine Working Group for introducing me to the Frame, Find, Evaluate and Apply steps of Evidence-Based Medicine.

Many thanks to my mother and father, Yvonne and Bernard Friedland, who taught me the value of love, the importance of family and making good decisions in my life.

I'm thankful for Dylan, the creator in our family. I love you with all my heart, son. Along with Zach, forever know you are the best decision mom and I ever made.

I'm thankful to Sue, my wife and loving partner, who walked across the dance floor to ask me to salsa dance with her. This book is largely a credit to Sue, who has spent countless hours framing, editing and reorganizing the content. In addition she took the picture of Zach and me on the cover of the book. In my heart I knew we could create a life together and am deeply appreciative for all she has done to inspire and support me to share my purpose with others.

And to Zach, I so appreciate working on this book with you. Words cannot fully express the depth of love I feel for you and how thankful I am that you are open to receiving what I have to share with you. I watch in awe at the phenomenal man you're becoming.

My ultimate appreciation belongs to the Source of inspiration that has inspired my life and this work and has blessed me with my family and a purpose to share.

REFERENCES

1. Goleman, D., *Social Intelligence*. 2006: Bantam.

2. Goleman, D., *Emotional Intelligence*. 2010: Bloomsbury Paperbacks.

3. Goleman, D., *The Brain and Emotional Intelligence: New Insights* 2011: More Than Sound LLC.

4. Siegel, D.J., *The Mindful Brain: Reflection and Attunement in the Cultivation of Well-Being*. 2007: W. W. Norton & Company.

5. Pillay, S.S., *Your Brain and Business: The Neuroscience of Great Leaders* 2011: FT Press.

6. Carson, S., *Your Creative Brain*. 2010: Harvard Health Publications and Jossey-Bass.

7. Porges, S.W., *The polyvagal theory: new insights into adaptive reactions of the autonomic nervous system*. Cleve Clin J Med, 2009. 76 Suppl 2: p. S86-90.

8. Twain, M. Cited 2013; Available from: http://www.thequotefactory.com/quote-by/mark-twain/ive-had-a-lot-of-worries-in-my/54563.

9. Kross, E., et al., *Social rejection shares somatosensory representations with physical pain.* Proc Natl Acad Sci U S A, 2011. 108(15): p. 6270-5.

10. Eisenberger, N.I., *The neural bases of social pain: evidence for shared representations with physical pain.* Psychosom Med, 2012. 74(2): p. 126-35.

11. Eisenberger, N.I. and M.D. Lieberman, *Why rejection hurts: a common neural alarm system for physical and social pain.* Trends Cogn Sci, 2004. 8(7): p. 294-300.

12. Eisenberger, N.I., M.D. Lieberman, and K.D. Williams, *Does rejection hurt? An FMRI study of social exclusion.* Science, 2003. 302(5643): p. 290-2.

13. Eisenlohr-Moul, T.A., M.T. Fillmore, and S.C. Segerstrom, *"Pause and plan" includes the liver: self-regulatory effort slows alcohol metabolism for those low in self-control.* Biol Psychol, 2012. 91(2): p. 229-31.

14. Segerstrom, S. *Pause and plan: Self-regulation and the heart.* 2012; Available from: http://psycnet.apa.org/index.cfm?fa=buy.optionToBuy&id=2011-09271-009.

15. McGonigal, K., *The Willpower Instinct.* 1st ed. 2011: Avery.

16. Schmitz, T.W., T.N. Kawahara-Baccus, and S.C. Johnson, *Metacognitive evaluation, self-relevance, and the right prefrontal cortex.* Neuroimage, 2004. 22(2): p. 941-7.

17. Rosenbloom, M.H., J.D. Schmahmann, and B.H. Price, *The functional neuroanatomy of decision-making.* J Neuropsychiatry Clin Neurosci, 2012. 24(3): p. 266-77.

18. Sapolsky, R.M., *The frontal cortex and the criminal*

justice system. Philos Trans R Soc Lond B Biol Sci, 2004. 359(1451): p. 1787-96.

19. Lieberman, M.D., et al., *Putting feelings into words: affect labeling disrupts amygdala activity in response to affective stimuli*. Psychol Sci, 2007. 18(5): p. 421-8.

20. Creswell, J.D., et al., *Neural correlates of dispositional mindfulness during affect labeling*. Psychosom Med, 2007. 69(6): p. 560-5.

21. Ochsner, K.N., et al., *Rethinking feelings: an FMRI study of the cognitive regulation of emotion*. J Cogn Neurosci, 2002. 14(8): p. 1215-29.

22. Modinos, G., J. Ormel, and A. Aleman, *Individual differences in dispositional mindfulness and brain activity involved in reappraisal of emotion*. Soc Cogn Affect Neurosci, 2010. 5(4): p. 369-77.

23. Davidson, R.J., et al., *Alterations in brain and immune function produced by mindfulness meditation*. Psychosom Med, 2003. 65(4): p. 564-70.

24. Chiesa, A. and A. Serretti, *A systematic review of neurobiological and clinical features of mindfulness meditations*. Psychol Med, 2010. 40(8): p. 1239-52.

25. Doidge, N., *The Brain That Changes Itself*. 2007: Penguin Books.

26. Jeffrey Schwartz, S.B., *The mind and the brain: neuroplasticity and the power of mental force*. 2002: Harper Collins.

27. Kabat-Zinn, J., *Full Catastrophe Living: Using the Wisdom of Your Body and Mind to Face Stress, Pain, and Illness*. 1990: Delta.

28. Kabat-Zinn, J., *Coming to Our Senses: Healing Ourselves and the World Through Mindfulness*. 2006: Hyperion.

29. Hofmann, S.G., et al., *The effect of mindfulness-based therapy on anxiety and depression: A meta-analytic review.* J Consult Clin Psychol, 2010. 78(2): p. 169-83.

30. Zylowska, L., et al., *Mindfulness meditation training in adults and adolescents with ADHD: a feasibility study.* J Atten Disord, 2008. 11(6): p. 737-46.

31. Alberts, H.J., R. Thewissen, and L. Raes, *Dealing with problematic eating behaviour. The effects of a mindfulness-based intervention on eating behaviour, food cravings, dichotomous thinking and body image concern.* Appetite, 2012.

32. Courbasson, C.M., Y. Nishikawa, and L.B. Shapira, *Mindfulness-Action Based Cognitive Behavioral Therapy for concurrent Binge Eating Disorder and Substance Use Disorders.* Eat Disord, 2011. 19(1): p. 17-33.

33. Hoppes, K., *The application of mindfulness-based cognitive interventions in the treatment of co-occurring addictive and mood disorders.* CNS Spectr, 2006. 11(11): p. 829-51.

34. Garland, E.L., et al., *Therapeutic mechanisms of a mindfulness-based treatment for IBS: effects on visceral sensitivity, catastrophizing, and affective processing of pain sensations.* J Behav Med, 2011.

35. Gaylord, S.A., et al., *Mindfulness training reduces the severity of irritable bowel syndrome in women: results of a randomized controlled trial.* Am J Gastroenterol, 2011. 106(9): p. 1678-88.

36. Ljotsson, B., et al., *Internet-delivered exposure and*

mindfulness based therapy for irritable bowel syndrome—a randomized controlled trial. Behav Res Ther, 2010. 48(6): p. 531-9.

37. Kabat-Zinn, J., et al., *Influence of a mindfulness meditation-based stress reduction intervention on rates of skin clearing in patients with moderate to severe psoriasis undergoing phototherapy (UVB) and photochemotherapy (PUVA).* Psychosom Med, 1998. 60(5): p. 625-32.

38. Grossman, P., et al., *Mindfulness training as an intervention for fibromyalgia: evidence of postintervention and 3-year follow-up benefits in well-being.* Psychother Psychosom, 2007. 76(4): p. 226-33.

39. Sampalli, T., et al., *A controlled study of the effect of a mindfulness-based stress reduction technique in women with multiple chemical sensitivity, chronic fatigue syndrome, and fibromyalgia.* J Multidiscip Healthc, 2009. 2: p. 53-9.

40. Schmidt, S., et al., *Treating fibromyalgia with mindfulness-based stress reduction: results from a 3-armed randomized controlled trial.* Pain, 2011. 152(2): p. 361-9.

41. Sephton, S.E., et al., *Mindfulness meditation alleviates depressive symptoms in women with fibromyalgia: results of a randomized clinical trial.* Arthritis Rheum, 2007. 57(1): p. 77-85.

42. Dalen, J., et al., *Pilot study: Mindful Eating and Living (MEAL): weight, eating behavior, and psychological outcomes associated with a mindfulness-based intervention for people with obesity.* Complement Ther Med, 2010. 18(6): p. 260-4.

43. Daubenmier, J., et al., *Mindfulness Intervention for*

Stress Eating to Reduce Cortisol and Abdominal Fat among Overweight and Obese Women: An Exploratory Randomized Controlled Study. J Obes, 2011. 2011: p. 651936.

44. Chiesa, A. and A. Serretti, *Mindfulness-based interventions for chronic pain: a systematic review of the evidence.* J Altern Complement Med, 2011. 17(1): p. 83-93.

45. Fox, S.D., E. Flynn, and R.H. Allen, *Mindfulness meditation for women with chronic pelvic pain: a pilot study.* J Reprod Med, 2011. 56(3-4): p. 158-62.

46. Morone, N.E., C.M. Greco, and D.K. Weiner, *Mindfulness meditation for the treatment of chronic low back pain in older adults: a randomized controlled pilot study.* Pain, 2008. 134(3): p. 310-9.

47. Holzel, B.K., et al., *Stress reduction correlates with structural changes in the amygdala.* Soc Cogn Affect Neurosci, 2010. 5(1): p. 11-7.

48. Chiesa, A., R. Calati, and A. Serretti, *Does mindfulness training improve cognitive abilities? A systematic review of neuropsychological findings.* Clin Psychol Rev, 2011. 31(3): p. 449-64.

49. Chiesa, A. and A. Serretti, *Mindfulness-based stress reduction for stress management in healthy people: a review and meta-analysis.* J Altern Complement Med, 2009. 15(5): p. 593-600.

50. Daniel J. Friedland, e.a., *Evidence-Based Medicine: A Framework for Clinical Practice.* 1998: McGraw-Hill.

51. Sharon E. Straus, e.a., *Evidence-Based Medicine: How to Practice and Teach Evidence-Based Medicine.* 2005:

Churchill Livingstone.

52. Friedland, D. *How to Make Smarter Health Decisions*. 2008. Available from: http://supersmarthealth.com/.

53. Fink, G., *Stress Science: Neuroendocrinology*. 2009: Academic Press.

54. Everly, G.S.J. and J.M. Lating, *A Clinical Guide to the Treatment of the Human Stress Response* 2002: Springer.

55. Gershon, M., *The Second Brain : The Scientific Basis of Gut Instinct and a Groundbreaking New Understanding of Nervous Disorders of the Stomach and Intestines*. 1st ed. 1998: Harper.

56. Baumeister, R.F., et al., *Ego depletion: is the active self a limited resource?* J Pers Soc Psychol, 1998. 74(5): p. 1252-65.

57. Muraven, M., D.M. Tice, and R.F. Baumeister, *Self-control as limited resource: regulatory depletion patterns.* J Pers Soc Psychol, 1998. 74(3): p. 774-89.

58. Roy Baumeister, J.T., *Willpower: Rediscovering the Greatest Human Strength*. Reprint ed. 2012: Penguin Books.

Thank you for reading this book and sharing this journey with us.

*We hope it has inspired and empowered you
to make better life decisions.*

*If you'd like to continue the journey, get extra bonus material and
join our community to find and give support to others
in making better decisions,
please visit us at:*

TheBigDecisionBook.com

Made in the USA
San Bernardino, CA
23 November 2013